A Whack on the Side of the Head

By Roger von Oech

A Whack on the Side of the Head:
How You Can Be More Creative

A Kick in the Seat of the Pants:
Using Your Explorer, Artist, Judge,
& Warrior to Be More Creative

Roger von Oech's
Creative Whack Pack
64 Creative Thinking Strategies

A Whack on the Side of the Head

How You Can Be More Creative

Revised Edition

Roger von Oech

Illustrated by George Willett

U.S. GAMES SYSTEMS, INC.
Publishers   Stamford, CT 06902 USA

A WHACK ON THE SIDE OF THE HEAD
Revised Edition

Copyright © 1983, 1990 Roger von Oech, All Rights Reserved

This edition published by U.S. Games Systems, Inc.
179 Ludlow Street, Stamford, CT 06902 USA,
under special arrangement with Warner Books,
666 Fifth Avenue, New York, NY 10103 USA

Printed in the United States of America

11 10 9 8 7 6 5 4 3 2
00 99 98 97 96 95 94 93 92 91

Library of Congress Cataloging-In-Publication Data

Von Oech, Roger.
    A whack on the side of the head: how you can be more creative/
by Roger von Oech. — Rev. ed.

        p.   cm.
    Includes index.
    ISBN 0-88079-479-8
    1. Creative thinking.   2. Success.   I. Title.
BF408.V58 1990   89-49405
153.3'5—dc20   CIP

Cover Design by Anne Twomey
Cover Illustration by George Willett
Book Design by Roger von Oech
Typestyle: ITC Cheltenham

For information about Creative Think:
Box 7354 Menlo Park, California USA 94026

To Wendy, Athena, and Alex

Table of Contents

Preface x

A Whack on the Side of the Head 3

Mental Sex..........What Is Creative Thinking..........Mental Locks..........
Opening Mental Locks.........Getting Whacked..........Summary

1. The Right Answer 21

Learning How to Think...........Consequences.........The Second Right
Answer.........Change Your Question.........Summary

2. That's Not Logical 33

Soft and Hard Association Quiz.........Soft and Hard Thinking..........
The Creative Process..........That's Not Logical...........Making the
Strange Familiar...........The Water Model of Finance........... Proverbs
..........The Meaning of Life...........Summary

3. Follow the Rules 53

Patterns: The Rules of the Game..........Challenging the Rules..........
Follow the Rules...........The Aslan Phenomenon..........Slay A Sacred
Cow...........Summary

4. Be Practical 67

Our Imaginative Seedbed..........What If?..........Imagine How Others
Would Do It...........Imagine You're the Idea..........The Stepping Stone
..........Be Practical..........Summary

5. Play Is Frivolous 87

The Moment of Conception.........Laugh At It ....Have Fun..........
The Moebius Stepping Stone..........Twelve-Sided Fun......... Summary

6. That's Not My Area 101
The Solar Cell..........That's Not My Area...........Cross-Fertilization
..........Be An Explorer..........Summary

7. Avoid Ambiguity 113
Thinking Ambiguously.........Paradoxes...........Consult An Oracle
..........Listen to Your Dreams..........Heraclitus..........Summary

8. Don't Be Foolish 133
Going Along...........Benefits of Conformity..........Groupthink...........
Consult A Fool...........Put On Your Fool's Cap..........Reverse Your
Viewpoint.........The Fools and the Rules..........Summary

9. To Err Is Wrong 151
Hits and Misses...........A Different Logic...........Is Failure Bad?...........
Is Success Good?..........Flex Your Risk Muscle...........Summary

10. I'm Not Creative 161
Self-Fulfilling Prophecies.......... Summary

A Whack on the Other Side of the Head 169
The Return Visit to the Creativity Teacher..........Be Dissatsified........
Map Out Your Plans..........Take A Whack At It..........Get Support........
Have Something At Stake........Get Rid of Excuses.......Be Courageous
..........Give Yourself A Deadline..........Fight For It..........Be Persistent

Examination 184

About the Author 192

Index of Proper Names 194

Preface

Eight years ago, I wrote the first edition of this book. It represented some of my basic ideas about the creative process, namely that creativity is fun, necessary, and accessible to all of us. Since then, I've been overwhelmed by the response, not only from North America but from around the world. Again and again, I've received letters from the United States and Canada as well as Japan, Australia, China, India, Europe, the Soviet Union, and South America saying "thanks for sparking my thinking."

If creative thinking was an important survival skill in the 1980's, it's even more important in the nineties. In almost every endeavor, it will be imperative to go beyond what worked in the past, and to come up with new approaches. The first edition of *Whack* was oriented toward a business audience. The majority of my letters, however, have come from a non-business audience: teachers, students, ministers, public servants, military personnel, prisoners, retired people, as well as business people. I've come to the conclusion that its message is applicable to all walks of life.

There is one audience in particular that I wish to reach with this new edition. Not long ago, I gave a speech at the Minneapolis Press Club. At the end of my talk, I received a question that went something like, "I want you to play visionary and look out into the future. What do you see?" I thought for a little bit and then said, "I bet you want an answer that deals with computers, robots, and biotechnology. However, I think that the real need for creativity is in our basic institutions—especially in the family and in the schools. That's where it needs to be cultivated." I think that anyone who graduates from high school who isn't able to write a cogent paragraph or balance a checkbook—basic critical thinking skills—has been greatly disserviced by their school system. By the same token, I think that because the world is continually changing, students—indeed all people–need creative thinking skills. These creative thinking skills must be encouraged and developed.

This book provides the fundamentals of creative thinking. Whether you're a junior in high school, an account executive at an advertising agency, a software programmer, or a mother raising a family, I think that you'll find some useful ideas in these pages.

I'd like to thank the following people who have made a difference in this book: Nansey Neiman, Bill Shinker, Larry Kirschbaum, Ling Lucas, Nancy Parker, Kathy Seligman, Bob Wieder, Metcalfe, Lance Shaw, Wiley Caldwell, Dan Zadra, and Doug King.

Many thanks to George Willett for his illustrations.

Most of all, I'd like to thank my wife Wendy for her ideas and encouragement.

Good Luck and Happy Whacking!

Roger von Oech
Atherton, California
New Year's Day 1990

A Whack on the Side of the Head

Mental Sex

Exercise: In my seminars, I like to start the participants off with the following exercise. Take a moment to do it.

1. When was the last time you came up with a creative idea?

☐ This morning
☐ Yesterday
☐ Last week
☐ Last month
☐ Last year

2. What was it?

3. What motivates you to be creative?

The answers I get usually run something like this: "I found a way to debug a software program"; "I thought up a new fund-raising strategy for our school"; "I discovered a way to sell a new application to a hard-to-satisfy client"; "I developed a new geometry curriculum"; "I motivated my daughter to do her homework"; or, "I decorated the living room around a different color."

Not long ago, I met a man who told me that he got his last creative idea a year ago. "This must have been *some* idea to have overshadowed everything else this year," I thought to myself, and asked him what it was. "I found a quicker way home from work," he replied.

I guess this person wasn't very motivated. He seemed to be

saying, "Everything is fine," and there's no reason to deviate from what's worked in the past. But he made me think: why be creative? Why challenge the rules? Why run the risk of failing and looking foolish?

I can think of two good reasons. The first is change. When things change and new information comes into existence, it's no longer possible to solve today's problems with yesterday's solutions. Over and over again, people are finding out that what worked two years ago won't work right now. This gives them a choice. They can either bemoan the fact that things aren't as easy as they used to be, or they can use their creative abilities to find new answers, new solutions, and new ideas.

A second reason for generating ideas is that it's a lot of fun. Indeed, I like to think of creative thinking as the "sex of our mental lives." Ideas, like organisms, have a life cycle. They are born, they develop, they reach maturity, and they die. So we need a way to generate new ideas. Creative thinking is that means, and like its biological counterpart, it's also pleasurable.

What Is Creative Thinking?

I once asked advertising legend Carl Ally what makes the creative person tick. Ally responded, "The creative person wants to be a know-it-all. He wants to know about all kinds of things: ancient history, nineteenth century mathematics, current manufacturing techniques, flower arranging, and hog futures. Because he never knows when these ideas might come together to form a new idea. It may happen six minutes later or six years down the road. But he has faith that it will happen."

I agree wholeheartedly. Knowledge is the stuff from which new ideas are made. Nonetheless, knowledge alone won't make a person creative. I think that we've all known people who knew lots of facts and nothing creative happened. Their knowledge just sat in their crania because they didn't think about what they knew in any new ways. The real key to being creative lies in what you do with your knowledge.

Creative thinking requires an attitude that allows you to search for ideas and manipulate your knowledge and experience. With this outlook, you try various approaches, first one, then another, often not getting anywhere. You use crazy, foolish, and impractical ideas as stepping stones to practical new ideas. You break the rules occasionally, and explore for ideas in unusual outside places. In short, by adopting a creative outlook you open yourself up both to new possibilities and to change.

A good example of a person who did this is Johann Gutenberg. What Gutenberg did was combine two previously unconnected ideas: the wine press and the coin punch. The purpose of the coin punch was to leave an image on a small area such as a gold coin. The function of the wine press was, and still is, to apply force over a large area to squeeze the juice out of grapes. One day, Gutenberg, perhaps after he'd drunk a goblet or two of wine, playfully asked himself, "What if I took a bunch of these coin punches and put them under the force of the wine press so that they left their image on paper?" The resulting combination was the printing press and movable type.

Navy Admiral Grace Hopper had the task of explaining the

meaning of a "nanosecond" to some non-technical computer users. (A nanosecond is a billionth of a second, and it's the basic time interval of a supercomputer's internal clock.) She wondered, "How can I get them to understand the brevity of a nanosecond? Why not look at it as a space problem rather than a time problem? I'll just use the distance light travels in one billionth of a second." She pulled out a piece of string 30 centi- meters long (11.8 inches) and told her visitors, "Here is one nanosecond."

In 1792, the musicians of Franz Joseph Haydn's orchestra got mad because the Duke promised them a vacation, but con- tinually postponed it. They asked Haydn to talk to the Duke about getting some time off. Haydn thought for a bit, decided to let music do the talking, and then wrote the "Farewell Sym- phony." The performance began with a full orchestra, but as the piece went along, it was scored to need fewer and fewer instruments. As each musician finished his part, he blew out his candle and left the stage. They did this, one by one, until the stage was empty. The Duke got the message and gave them a vacation.

Then there's Pablo Picasso. One day, he went outside his house and found an old bicycle. He looked at it for a little bit and took off the seat and the handle bars. Then then welded them together to create the head of a bull.

Each of these examples illustrates the creative mind's power to transform one thing into another. By changing per- spective and playing with our knowledge, we can make the ordinary extraordinary and the unusual commonplace. In this way, wine presses squeeze out information, string is trans- formed into nanoseconds, labor grievances become sympho- nies, and bicycle seats turn into bulls' heads.

The Nobel prize winning physician Albert Szent-Györgyi put it well when he said:

Discovery consists of looking at the same thing as everyone else and thinking something different.

Here are four quick exercises to give you a chance to "think something different."

Exercise: An eccentric old king wants to give his throne to one of his two sons. He decides that a horse race will be run and the son who owns the slower horse will become king. The sons, each fearing that the other will cheat by having his horse run less fast than it is capable, ask the court fool for his advice. With only two words the fool tells them how to make sure that the race will be fair. What are the two words?

Exercise: What is this figure?

Exercise: Can you think of a way in which you put a sheet of newspaper on the floor so that when two people stand face to face on it, they won't be able to touch one another? Cutting or tearing the paper is not allowed. Neither is tying up the people or preventing them from moving.

Exercise: Shown on the top of the next page is the Roman numeral seven. By adding only a single line, turn it into an eight.

VII

This is pretty easy; all you have to do is add a vertical line to the right of the VII to create an eight—like so—VIII. Want something a little more challenging? Shown below is a Roman numeral nine. By adding only a single line, turn it into a 6.

IX

Some people put a horizontal line through the center, turn it upside down, and then cover the bottom. This gives you a Roman numeral VI. But if you're "thinking something different," you might put an "S" in front of the IX to create "SIX." What you have done is take the IX out of the context of Roman numerals and put it into the context of Arabic numerals spelled out in English. The thing that prevents some people from doing this is that even with only three examples of Roman numerals—VII, VIII, and IX—they get locked into the context of Roman numerals.

Let's look for a second right answer. Can you think of any other ways in which you can add a single line to "IX" and turn it into a 6?

IX

Another solution might be to add the line "6" after IX. Then you get IX6, or one times six. Here the "X" no longer represents "10" or the English letter "X" but rather the multiplication sign. The point is this: everybody has a lot of knowledge; by shifting contexts in which you think about it, you'll discover new ideas.

(Switch horses. If you look at it one way, it's a bird. If you look at it another way, it could be a question mark. If you turn it upside down, it looks like a seal juggling a ball on its nose. Try putting the newspaper in a doorway–door closed–with the two people standing on each side.)

Mental Locks

Why don't we "think something different" more often? There are several main reasons. The first is that we don't need to be creative for most of what we do. For example, we don't need to be creative when we're driving on the freeway, or riding in an elevator, or waiting in line at a grocery store. We are creatures of habit when it comes to the business of living—everything from doing paperwork to tying our shoes to haggling with telephone solicitors.

For most of our activities, these routines are indispensable. Without them, our lives would be in chaos, and we wouldn't get much accomplished. If you got up this morning and started contemplating the bristles on your toothbrush or questioning the meaning of toast, you probably wouldn't make it to work. Staying on routine thought paths enables us to do the many things we need to do without having to think about them.

Another reason we're not more creative is that we haven't been taught to be. Much of our educational system is an elaborate game of "guess what the teacher is thinking." Many of us have been taught to think that the best ideas are in someone else's head. How many of your teachers asked you, "What original ideas do you have?"

There are times, however, when you need to be creative and generate new ways to accomplish your objectives. When this happens, your own belief systems may prevent you from doing so. Here we come to a third reason why we don't "think something different" more often. Most of us have certain attitudes that lock our thinking into the status quo and keep us thinking "more of the same." These attitudes are necessary for most of what we do, but they can get in the way when we're trying to be creative.

I call these attitudes *mental locks*. There are ten mental locks in particular that I've found to be especially hazardous to our thinking. They are listed on the next page.

As you can well imagine, it's difficult to get your creative juices flowing if you're always being practical, following rules, afraid to make mistakes, not looking into outside areas, or under the influence of any other mental lock.

1. The Right Answer.

2. That's Not Logical.

3. Follow the Rules.

4. Be Practical.

5. Play Is Frivolous.

6. That's Not My Area.

7. Avoid Ambiguity.

8. Don't Be Foolish.

9. To Err Is Wrong.

10. I'm Not Creative.

Opening Mental Locks

So, how do we open these mental locks? Let's turn to the following story for a possible answer.

> A creativity teacher invited one of his students over to his house for afternoon tea. They talked for a bit, and then came time for tea. The teacher poured some into the student's cup. Even after the cup was full, he continued to pour. The cup overflowed and tea spilled out onto the floor.
>
> Finally, the student said: "Master, you must stop pouring; the tea is overflowing—it's not going into the cup."
>
> The teacher replied, "That's very observant. The same is true with you. If you are to receive any of my teachings, you must first empty out what you have in your mental cup."
>
> *Moral:* We need the ability to unlearn what we know.

From our examples, we can see that Gutenberg forgot that wine presses only squeeze grapes—the "right answer"; Hopper didn't realize that everyday package-string was "outside the area" of supercomputing; Haydn didn't understand that equating music and labor grievances was a "foolish" idea; and Picasso broke the "rule" that bicycle seats are for sitting on.

Without the ability to temporarily forget what we know, our minds remain cluttered with ready-made answers, and we never have an opportunity to ask the questions that lead off the beaten path in new directions. Since the attitudes that create mental locks have all been learned, one key to opening them is to temporarily unlearn them—to empty our mental cup.

This sounds like a simple technique, but sometimes it's difficult to apply. Often we have integrated these mental locks so

well into our thinking and behavior that we are no longer aware that we're being guided by them. They have become habits. The danger of habits is that a person can become a prisoner of familiarity. The more often you do something in the same way—whether it's cooking a meal or managing a project —the more difficult it is to do it in any other way. You get stuck in how you already think about things.

So, sometimes we need a little extra assistance to open the mental locks. Let's return to our creativity teacher once more.

At another lesson the teacher and the student are discussing a problem. Despite lengthy conversation, the student doesn't seem to understand the point the teacher is making.

Finally, the teacher picks up a stick and gives a him a whack on the side of the head with it. Suddenly, the student begins to grasp the situation and "think something different."

Moral: Sometimes, nothing short of "a whack on the side of the head" can dislodge the assumptions that keep us thinking "more of the same."

Getting Whacked

Like the student, we all need an occasional whack on the side of the head to shake us out of routine patterns, to force us to re-think our problems, and to stimulate us to ask the questions that may lead to other right answers.

"Whacks" come in all shapes, sizes, and colors. They have one thing in common, however. They force you—at least for the moment—"to think something different." Sometimes you'll get whacked by a problem or a failure. Sometimes it'll be the result of a joke or a paradox. And sometimes it will be a surprise or an unexpected situation that whacks you. Here are some examples:

◆ It could result from your getting fired from a job, or failing to obtain a performance raise.

◆ It could happen when a teacher tells you that she thinks that you have a special talent in an area you'd never thought much about and assigns a project—due next Friday—to help you develop it.

◆ It might happen when the supplier for a vital sub-component of your best selling product unexpectedly goes on strike and you're forced to scramble to find a new source. When the dust has cleared you discover that the new vendor is far superior in product quality.

◆ It could come when you recognize a relationship between two things you thought were unconnected such as a spiral galaxy and a spinning ice skater.

◆ It could happen when you observe the second hand of your watch in a mirror. (Try it!)

◆ It could be the result of traveling to another country, say England, and being forced to drive on the left side of the road.

◆ It could happen when you break your leg and you realize how much you took your ambulatory habits for granted.

◆ It could happen when someone tells you that the answer to your problem is the seventh word down on page 237 of your dictionary, and when you look it up, you discover that she's right.

◆ It could be a question you never thought about:

    ❧ "What's the rationale behind many cars having two keys—one for the door and the other for the ignition?"

    ❧ "Is the pushbutton telephone the death of the word 'dialing'?"

    ❧ "If camels are the ships of the desert' why aren't tugboats the 'camels of the sea'?"

    ❧ "If you put an orchid in your refrigerator and a day later it starts smelling like salami, does the salami start smelling like an orchid?"

    ❧ "Do sportcasters in India yell, 'Holy Cow'?"

    ❧ "If we call oranges 'oranges', why don't we call bananas 'yellows,' or apples 'reds'?"

◆ It could be a joke:

    Q: What is the difference between a cat and a comma?

    A: A cat has its claws at the end of its paws and a comma is the pause at the end of a clause.

◆ It might happen when you find out that the "nerd" in your high school class has become a millionaire through speculating in the commodities market.

    Those ideas or situations that cause you to get off your routine paths and "think something different" are whacks to your thinking.

    Sometimes getting a whack on the side of the head can be the best thing to happen to you. It might help you spot a potential problem before it arises. It could help you discover an opportunity that wasn't previously apparent. Or, it could help you generate some new ideas.

    Thomas Edison serves as a good example for the benefits of getting whacked. As a young man, his primary interest was improving the telegraph. He invented the multi-plex telegraph, the ticker tape machine (a variation of the telegraph), and other telegraphic innovations. Then, in the early 1870's, the financier Jay Gould bought out the Western Union telegraph system thereby establishing a monopoly over the industry. Edison realized that as long as Gould owned the system, the need to be innovative was reduced. This whacked him out of his telegraphic routine, and forced him to look for other ways in which to use his talent. Within a few years, he came up with the light bulb, the power plant, the phonograph, the film projector, and many other inventions. He may have discovered these anyway, but Gould's whack was certainly a stimulant in getting him to look for other opportunities.

A more recent example is Rex McPherson—a third-generation citrus grower in central Florida. In the early 1980's, he lost 85% of his citrus stock due to severe freezes two consecutive years. This loss forced him to re-think his whole citrus-growing concept. Rex realized that the trees (planted by his grandfather in the 1930's and 1940's) had been placed fairly far apart because land at that time was cheap. Land values have skyrocketed since then. He decided to use new hybrids and irrigation techniques to plant the trees close together. As a result, not only has his yield increased significantly, but also the closeness of the trees has helped to inhibit freezing. The whack (the loss due to the freezes) was painful at the time, but it provided Rex with the impetus to "think something different."

Here's a personal whack. Several years ago, the pool where my Masters swimming team works out was closed for a month of maintenance. During the downtime, the members had to practice with other clubs in the area. When we were re-united a month later, there was a great outpouring of new workout ideas. One person had been with a team that had low rest-interval workout. Another came back with a heartbeat interval workout. Another found a new type of ankle pull-buoy. All these ideas were discovered because we were forced to break our routine.

Summary

We don't need to be creative for most of what we do, but when there is a need to "think something different," our own attitudes can get in the way. I call these attitudes *mental locks*.

Mental locks can be opened in one of two ways. The first technique is to become aware of them, and then to temporarily forget them when you are trying to generate new ideas. If that doesn't work, maybe you need a "whack on the side of the head." That should dislodge the presuppositions that hold the locks in place.

For the remainder of the book, we'll examine each of the mental locks and find out what kinds of ideas can be generated by temporarily opening them. We'll also take a look at some techniques to whack our thinking. Along the way we'll meet some interesting head-whackers: artists, poets, revolutionaries, magicans, explorers, fools, and self-trusting innovators.

Let's Get Rolling!

1. The Right Answer

Exercise: Five figures are shown below. Select the one that is different from all the others.

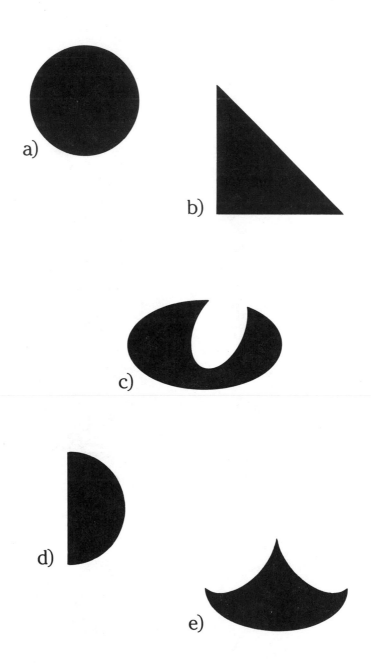

Learning How to Think

Children enter school as question marks and leave as periods.
—Neil Postman, Educator

Life can be like a big noisy party with people talking, music playing, and glasses clinking. But even with all of this noise, it's possible for you to understand the person across from you. Or the one thirty feet away. That's because our attention is selective–we can tune in certain things and tune out others.

See for yourself. Take a look around where you're sitting and find four things that have "red" in them. Go ahead and do it.

With a "red" mindset, you'll find that red jumps right out at you: a red telephone book, red in the blister on your index finger, red in the wallpaper, and so on. Similarly, whenever you learn a new word, you hear it eight times in the next three days. In like fashion, you've probably noticed that after you get a new car, you see that make everywhere. That's because people find what they're looking for. If you're looking for beauty, you'll find beauty. If you're looking for conspiracies, you'll find conspiracies. It's all a matter of setting your mental channel.

Where do you learn how to set your mental channel? One important source is your formal education. There you learn what is appropriate and what is not. You learn many of the questions you use to probe your surroundings. You learn where to search for information, which ideas to pay attention to, and how to think about these ideas. Your educational training gives you many of the concepts you use to order and understand the world.

Speaking of education, how did you do on the five-figure exercise on the previous page? If you chose figure B, congratulations! You've picked the right answer. Figure B is the only one that has all straight lines. Give yourself a pat on the back!

Some of you, however, may have chosen figure C, thinking that C is unique because it's the only one that is asymmetrical. And you are also right! C is the right answer. A case can also be made for figure A: it's the only one with no points. Therefore, A is the right answer. What about D? It is the only one that has both a straight line and a curved line. So, D is the right answer too. And E? Among other things, E is the only one that looks like a projection of a non-Euclidean triangle into Euclidean space. It is also the right answer. In other words, they are all right depending on your point of view.

But you won't find this exercise in school. Much of our educational system is geared toward teaching people to find "the right answer." By the time the average person finishes college, he or she will have taken over 2,600 tests, quizzes, and exams—many similar to the one you just took. The "right answer" approach becomes deeply ingrained in our thinking. This may be fine for some mathematical problems where there is in fact only one right answer. The difficulty is that most of life isn't this way. Life is ambiguous; there are many right answers—all depending what you are looking for. But if you think there is only one right answer, then you'll stop looking as soon as you find one.

When I was a sophomore in high school, my English teacher put a small chalk dot like the one below on the blackboard.

She asked the class what it was. A few seconds passed and then someone said, "A chalk dot on the blackboard." The rest of the class seemed relieved that the obvious had been stated, and no one else had anything more to say. "I'm surprised at you," the teacher told the class. "I did the same exercise yesterday with a group of kindergartners and they thought of fifty different things it could be: an owl's eye, a cigar butt, the top of a telephone pole, a star, a pebble, a squashed bug, a rotten egg, and so on. They really had their imaginations in high gear."

In the ten year period between kindergarten and high school, not only had we learned how to find the right answer, we had also lost the ability to look for more than one right answer. We had learned how to be specific, but we had lost much of our imaginative power.

An elementary school teacher told me the following story about a colleague who had given her first graders a coloring assignment:

> The instructions said: "On this sheet of paper, you will find an outline of a house, trees, flowers, clouds and sky. Please color each with the appropriate colors."
>
> One of the students, Patty, put a lot of work into her drawing. When she got it back, she was surprised to find a big black "X" on it. She asked the teacher for an explanation. "I gave you an 'X' because you didn't follow instructions. Grass is green, not gray. The sky should be blue, not yellow as you have drawn it. Why didn't you use the normal colors, Patty?"
>
> Patty answered, "Because that's how it looks to me when I get up early to watch the sunrise."

The teacher had assumed that there was only one right answer.

Consequences

"I'm not returning until you fix it," bandleader Count Basie told a nightclub owner whose piano was always out of tune. A month later Basie got a call that everything was fine. When he returned, the piano was still out of tune. "You said you fixed it!" an irate Basie exclaimed. "I did," came the reply. "I had it painted."

The practice of looking for the "right answer" can have serious consequences in the way we think about and deal with problems. Most people don't like problems, and when they encounter them, they usually react by taking the first way out they can find—even if they solve the wrong problem as did the nightclub owner in the above story. I can't overstate the danger in this. If you have only one idea, you have only one course of action open to you, and this is quite risky in a world where flexibility is a requirement for survival.

An idea is like a musical note. In the same way that a musical note can only be understood in relation to other notes (either as a part of a melody or a chord), an idea is best understood in the context of other ideas. If you have only one idea you don't have anything to compare it to. You don't know its strengths and weaknesses. I believe that the French philosopher Emilé Chartier hit the nail squarely on the head when he said:

Nothing is more dangerous than an idea when it's the only one you have.

For more effective thinking, we need different points of view. Otherwise, we'll get stuck looking at the same things and miss seeing things outside our focus.

The Second Right Answer

A leading business school did a study that showed that its graduates performed well at first, but in ten years, they were overtaken by a more streetwise, pragmatic group. The reason according to the professor who ran the study: "We taught them how to solve problems, not recognize opportunities. When opportunity knocked, they put out their 'Do Not Disturb' signs."

Not long ago I did a series of creative thinking workshops for the executive staff of a large computer company. The president had called me in because he was concerned about the stagnant thinking environment at the top. It seemed that whenever his subordinates would make a proposal, that's all they'd make—just one. They wouldn't offer any alternative ideas. Since they had been trained to look for the right answer, they usually didn't go beyond the first one they found. The president knew that it was easier to make good decisions if he had a variety of ideas from which to choose. He was also concerned with how conservative this "one-idea" tendency had made his people's thinking. If a person were presenting only one idea, he would generally propose the "sure thing" rather than take a chance on a less likely off-beat idea. This state of affairs created a less than ideal climate for generating innovative ideas. I told them that one way to be more creative is to:

Look for the second right answer.

Often, it is the second right answer which, although off-beat or unusual, is exactly what you need to solve a problem in an innovative way.

One technique for finding the second right answer is to change the questions you use to probe a problem. For example, how many times have you heard someone say, "What is the answer?" or "What is the meaning of this?" or "What is the result?" These people are looking for *the* answer, and *the* meaning, and *the* result. And that's all they'll find—just one. If you train yourself to ask questions that solicit plural answers like "What are the answers?" or "What are the meanings?" or "What are the results?" you will find that people will think a little more deeply and offer more than one idea. As the Nobel Prize winning chemist Linus Pauling put it:

The best way to get a good idea is to get a lot of ideas.

You may not be able to use all of them, but out of the number you generate you may find a few that are worthwhile. This is why professional photographers take so many pictures when shooting an important subject. They may take twenty, sixty or a hundred shots. They'll change the exposure, the lighting, the filters, and so on. That's because they know that out of all the pictures they take, there may be only a few that capture what they're looking for. It's the same thing with creative thinking: you need to generate a lot of ideas to get some good ones.

Inventor Ray Dolby (the man who took "hiss" out of recorded music) has a similar philosophy. He says:

> Inventing is a skill that some people have and some people don't. But you can learn how to invent. You have to have the will not to jump at the first solution because the really elegant solution might be right around the corner. An inventor is someone who says, "Yes, that's one way to do it, but it doesn't seem to be an optimum solution." Then he keeps on thinking.

When you look for more than one right answer, you allow your imagination to open up. How do you keep a fish from smelling? Cook it as soon as you catch it. Freeze it. Wrap it in paper. Leave it in the water. Switch to chicken. Keep a cat around. Burn incense. Cut its nose off.

Change Your Question

The second assault on the same problem should come from a totally different direction.
—Tom Hirshfield, Physicist

Another technique for finding more answers is to change the wording in your questions. If an architect looks at an opening between two rooms and thinks, "What type of *door* should I use to connect these rooms?" that's what he'll design—a door. But if he thinks "What sort of *passageway* should I put here?" he may design something different like a "hallway," an "air curtain," a "tunnel," or perhaps a "courtyard." Different words bring in different assumptions and lead your thinking in different directions.

Here's an example of how such a strategy can work. Several centuries ago, a curious but deadly plague appeared in a small village in Lithuania. What was curious about this disease was its grip on its victim; as soon as a person contracted it, he'd go into a deep almost deathlike coma. Most died within a day, but occasionally a hardy soul would make it back to the full bloom of health. The problem was that since eighteenth century medical technology wasn't very advanced, the unafflicted had quite a difficult time telling whether a victim was dead or alive.

Then one day it was discovered that someone had been buried alive. This alarmed the townspeople, so they called a town meeting to decide what should be done to prevent such a situation from happening again. After much discussion, most people agreed on the following solution. They decided to put food and water in every casket next to the body. They would even put an air hole from the casket up to the earth's surface. These procedures would be expensive, but they would be more than worthwhile if they would save people's lives.

Another group came up with a second, less expensive, right answer. They proposed implanting a twelve inch long stake in every coffin lid directly over where the victim's heart would be. Then whatever doubts there were about whether the person was dead or alive would be eliminated as soon the coffin lid was closed.

What differentiated the two solutions were the questions used to find them. Whereas the first group asked, "What should we do if we bury somebody *alive?*" the second group wondered, "How can we make sure everyone we bury is *dead?*"

The Sufi Judge

I'd like to conclude this "right answer" chapter with one of my favorite Sufi stories.

> Two men had an argument. To settle the matter, they went to a Sufi judge for arbitration. The plaintiff made his case. He was very eloquent and persuasive in his reasoning. When he finished, the judge nodded in approval and said, "That's right, that's right."
>
> On hearing this, the defendant jumped up and said, "Wait a second, judge, you haven't even heard my side of the case yet." So the judge told the defendant to state his case. He, too, was very persuasive and eloquent. When he finished, the judge said, "That's right, that's right."
>
> When the clerk of court heard this, he jumped up and said, "Judge, they both can't be right." The judge looked at the clerk and said, "That's right, that's right."

Moral: Truth is all around you; what matters is where you place your focus.

THAT'S RIGHT!

THAT'S RIGHT!

Summary

Much of our educational system has taught us to look for the one right answer. This approach is fine for some situations, but many of us have a tendency to stop looking for alternative right answers after the first right answer has been found. This is unfortunate because often it's the second, or third, or tenth right answer which is what we need to solve a problem in an innovative way.

There are many ways to find the second right answer— asking "what if," playing the fool, reversing the problem, breaking the rules, etc. Indeed, that's what much of this book is about. The important thing, however, is to look for the second right answer, because unless you do, you won't find it.

TIP: The answers you get depend on the questions you ask. Play with your wording to get different answers. One technique is to solicit plural answers. Another is to ask questions that whack people's thinking. One woman told me that she had a manager who would keep her mind on its toes by asking questions such as: "What are three things you feel totally neutral about?" and "What parts of your problem do you associate with tax returns and what parts with poetry?"

2. That's Not Logical

Exercise: Take a blank sheet of paper and draw a vertical line down the center. On the top left, write the word "Soft," and on the top right write the word "Hard." Now take a moment and look at the following concepts. Those you associate with being soft, put in the "Soft" column. Those you associate with being hard, put in the "Hard" column. This is a subjective exercise, but you should have a general feeling for soft and hard things.

Logic
Metaphor
Dream
Reason
Precision
Humor
Consistency
Ambiguity
Play
Work
Exact
Approximate
Direct
Focused
Fantasy
Reality
Paradox
Diffuse
Analysis
Hunch
Generalization
Specifics
Child
Adult

Now take a moment to think about this question: how would you compare the "Hard" list with the "Soft" one? Objective versus subjective? Quantitative versus qualitative? Masculine versus feminine?

Soft and Hard Thinking

At this point, you might be wondering about the purpose of this exercise. Well, the difference between soft and hard helped solve a problem for me. Not long ago, I stayed up late one night and tried to think of all the different types of thinking there are. Here's a partial list:

Logical thinking	Mythical thinking
Conceptual thinking	Poetic thinking
Analytical thinking	Non-verbal thinking
Speculative thinking	Elliptical thinking
Right brain thinking	Analogical thinking
Critical thinking	Lyrical thinking
Foolish thinking	Practical thinking
Convergent thinking	Divergent thinking
Weird thinking	Ambiguous thinking
Reflective thinking	Constructive thinking
Visual thinking	Thinking about thinking
Symbolic thinking	Surreal thinking
Propositional thinking	Focused thinking
Digital thinking	Concrete thinking
Metaphorical thinking	Fantasy thinking

I must have thought of close to a hundred different types of thinking. Then I asked myself, "How can I order them? What patterns do they have in common?" I thought about these questions for some time, but came up empty.

I was about to go to bed when I remembered the words of Kenneth Boulding. Boulding is an economist by profession, but more than that, he is a student of life. What Boulding said was this:

There are two kinds of people in this world: those who divide everything into two groups, and those who don't.

At that moment I was feeling like a member of the former group. I thought: "Why not apply this binary insight to the different types of thinking and divide them into two groups." But what would the differentiating factors be? I thought of opposites: good/bad, strong/weak, inside/outside, big/small, masculine/feminine, living/dying, and so on, but none of these expressed what I was looking for. And then it hit me: why not *soft* and *hard*?

If you are like a lot of people, your "Soft" and "Hard" lists probably looked something like this:

Soft	**Hard**
Metaphor	Logic
Dream	Reason
Humor	Precision
Ambiguity	Consistency
Play	Work
Approximate	Exact
Fantasy	Reality
Paradox	Direct
Diffuse	Focused
Hunch	Analysis
Generalization	Specific
Child	Adult

As you can see, things on the hard side have a definite right and wrong answer; on the soft side, there may be many right answers. On the hard side, things are black and white; on the soft side there are many shades of gray (to say nothing of orange, purple, and magenta!). A few of you might say that you can pick up the things on the hard side—like a bar of metal. The soft things are a little more difficult to grab onto—like a handful of water.

Soft thinking has many of the characteristics on the "Soft" list: it is metaphorical, approximate, humorous, playful, and capable of dealing with contradiction. *Hard thinking,* on the other hand, tends to be more logical, precise, exact, specific, and consistent. We might say that hard thinking is like a spotlight. It is bright, clear, and intense, but the focus is narrow. Soft thinking is like a floodlight. It is more diffuse, not as intense, but covers a wider area.

Soft thinking tries to find similarities and connections among things, while hard thinking focuses on their differences. For example, a soft thinker might say that a cat and refrigerator have a lot in common, and then proceed to point out their similarities (they both have a place to put fish, they both have tails, they both come in a variety of colors, they both purr, they both have a lifetime of about fifteen years, etc.). The hard thinker would establish the cat and the refrigerator as being part of two different sets.

A person using soft thinking might ask a question such as, "What would furniture look like if our knees bent the other way?" The hard thinker would say, "What materials should be used in manufacturing to optimize the rate of return on this new line of chairs?"

The Creative Process

Where do you use soft and hard thinking? To answer this question, we should turn to the creative process. There are two main phases in the development of new ideas: an *imaginative* phase and a *practical* one.

In the imaginative phase, you generate and play with ideas. In the practical phase, you evaluate and execute them. To use a biological metaphor, the imaginative phase sprouts the new ideas and the practical phase cultivates and harvests them.

In the imaginative phase, you ask questions such as: What if? Why not? What rules can we break? What assumptions can we drop? How about if we looked at this backwards? Can we borrow a metaphor from another discipline? The motto of the imaginative phase is: *Thinking something different.*

In the practical phase, you ask questions such as: Is this idea any good? Do we have the resources to implement it? Is the timing right? Who can help us? What's the deadline? What are the consequences of not reaching the objective? The motto of the practical phase is: *Getting something done.*

Both types of thinking play an important role in the creative process, but usually during different phases. Soft thinking is quite effective in the imaginative phase when you are searching for new ideas, thinking globally, and manipulating problems. Hard thinking, on the other hand, is best used in the practical phase when you are evaluating ideas, narrowing in on practical solutions, running risk-analyses, and preparing to carry the idea into action.

A good analogy for the need for both types of thinking in the creative process is a potter making a vase. If you've ever done any work with clay, you know that it's a lot easier to shape, mold, and throw the clay if it has some softness to it (brittle clay is hard to shape). By the same token, after the vase has been shaped, it has no practical value until it has been put into a kiln and fired. Both the soft and the hard elements are required but at different times.

If soft and hard thinking have their respective strengths, they also have their weaknesses. Thus, it is important to know when each is *not* appropriate. Soft thinking in the practical phase can prevent the execution of an idea; here firmness and directness are preferable to ambiguity and dreams. Conversely, hard thinking in the imaginative phase can limit the creative process. Logic and analysis are important tools, but an over-reliance on them—especially early in the creative process—can prematurely narrow your thinking.

That's Not Logical

The first and supreme principle of traditional logic is the
law of non-contradiction. Logic can comprehend only those
things that have a consistent and non-contradictory nature.
This is fine except that most of life is ambiguous: inconsistency
and contradiction are the hallmarks of human existence. As a
result, the number of things that can be thought about in a
logical manner is small, and an overemphasis on the logical
method can inhibit your thinking.

Some people, however, have little use for soft thinking.
Their feeling toward it is "that's not logical." When faced with a
problem, they immediately bring in their hard thinking strategies. They say, "Let's get down to brass tacks." They never give
themselves an opportunity to consider steel tacks, copper
tacks, plastic tacks, sailing tacks, income tax, syntax, or con-
tacts. If you use a little soft thinking early in the creative process, you may still end up going with the "brass tacks," but at
least you will have considered alternatives.

Our educational system does a fairly good job of developing hard thinking skills, but there is not much to develop soft
thinking. As a matter of fact, much of our education is geared
toward eliminating soft thinking, or at best, teaching us to
regard it as an inferior tool. Human intelligence is a complicated phenomenon, and yet many of our formal notions of intelligence are based on logic and analysis. Musical ability,
decorating, painting, and cooking seem to have no place in
many test-makers' conception of intelligence. As creativity
educator Edward de Bono points out, if someone says he has
learned to think, most of us assume that he means he has
learned to think logically.

There is another reason for the "that's not logical" mental
lock. As an historian of ideas, I've noticed that the models
people use to understand mental processes reflect the technology of their time. For example, in the 17th century, people
thought about the mind as though it were a mirror or a lens,
and this "reflects" the advances made then in the fields of
optics and lens-making. The Freudian model of mind, devel-

oped in the late 19th and early 20th centuries, seems based on the ubiquity of the steam engine locomotive. Ideas billow up from the subconscious to the conscious in the same way steam moves from boiler to compression chamber. In the early twentieth century, the mind was viewed by some as a vast telephone switching network with circuits and relays running through the brain.

For the past thirty years, we've had a new model of mind: the computer. This model does a good job of describing certain aspects of our thinking. For example, we have "input" and "output" and "information processing." There is also "feedback," "programming," and "storage."

This is fine as far as it goes, but some people take this model literally and think that the mind really *is* a computer. Indeed, they may not only dismiss the soft types of thinking for not being "logical," but even treat other people like machines. How many times have you heard someone say, "I interface with that person," or "I'm operating in panic mode," or "I need to make an information dump on you"? The best one I heard was from a person describing the different parts of a computer system: "There is hardware, software, firmware, and liveware." Liveware is the people-element of the system.

I believe that the mind is not only a computer that processes information, it's also a museum that stores experiences, a device that encodes holograms, a playground in which to play, a muscle to be strengthened, a workshop in which to construct thoughts, a debating opponent to be won over, a cat to be stroked, a funhouse to be explored, a compost pile to be turned, and forty-three others. There are a lot of right ways to model the mind all depending on what you think is important.

One of the saddest consequences of the "that's not logical" mental lock is that its prisoner may not pay attention to one of the mind's softest and most valuable creations: the intuitive hunch. Your mind is constantly recording, connecting, and storing unrelated knowledge, experiences, and feelings. Later, it combines this disparate information into answers—hunches —to the problems you're facing, if you simply ask, trust, and listen. These hunches, for no apparent logical reason, might lead you to trying a different problem-solving approach, going out on a blind date, betting on the underdog in a sporting event, taking a spontaneous vacation, or ignoring a trusted friend's financial advice.

Exercise: What hunches have you had recently? Which ones did you listen to? How did things work out? What decision are you currently facing? What does your gut tell you to do?

Making the Strange Familiar

To combat the dangers of creative rigor mortis due to excessive hard thinking, I would like to introduce one of my favorite soft thinking tools. I'll introduce it with an exercise. As you do this exercise, think of yourself as a poet. This is a high compliment: our word poet comes from the classical Greek word *poietes* which meant not only "poet" but also "creator."

Exercise: What do the following have in common?

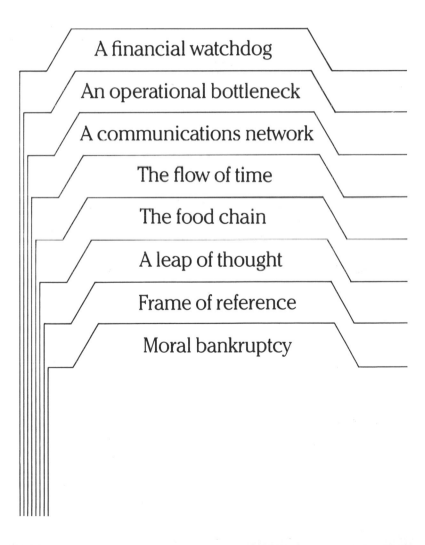

A financial watchdog

An operational bottleneck

A communications network

The flow of time

The food chain

A leap of thought

Frame of reference

Moral bankruptcy

The metaphor is probably the most fertile power possessed by man.

–Ortega y Gasset, Philosopher

In addition to everything else, they are all metaphors. They all connect two different universes of meaning through some similarity they share. In doing so, metaphors help us to understand one idea by means of another. For example, we understand the nature of a particular financial function by comparing it to a watchdog (they both protect), the passing of time to a river (flow), and the feeding interrelationship of the animal world to a chain (links).

The key to metaphorical thinking is similarity. In fact, this is how our thinking grows: we understand the unfamiliar by means of the similarities it has with what is familiar to us. For example, what were the first automobiles called? That's right, "horseless carriages." And the first locomotives were called "iron horses." We refer to resemblances between things all of the time. We say that hammers have "heads," tables have "legs," roads have "shoulders," cities have "hearts," and beds have "feet." It's all very soft, but it *is* how we think.

How about a metaphor for metaphors? Sure. Let's suppose that you fly to Salt Lake City, and that you've never been there before. You get off the airplane and rent a car. What's the first thing you should do? Probably get a map of the city to see how it's laid out, to find out where the freeways are, and to see where the sites are located. The map itself is not Salt Lake City, but it does give you a basic idea of the structure of the city. So, a metaphor is a mental map.

Metaphors are quite useful in helping you get a different slant on a problem. For example, in the early part of the twentieth century, Danish physicist Niels Bohr, developed a new model of the atom by comparing it to the solar system. Within this framework, he figured that the sun represented the nucleus and the planets represented the electrons.

Another example: several years ago I had a client whose sales were flat even though there was a boom in the marketplace for the products they offered. We decided to make a

metaphor for their company. We decided that their company
was like a full service restaurant. Its menu (product line) was
large, but there were many restrictions on what could be pur-
chased—for example, a customer couldn't order chili with veal.
Since the individual chefs (division managers) decided what
was on the menu, there was no consistency in their offerings.
This led to their having specialized waiters (salespeople). A
typical result? A customer couldn't buy pasta from a steak
waiter. We developed this metaphor further, but it quickly
became clear to us that the large, restricted product line confused their customers, and was the main source of their flat
sales.

Metaphors are also effective in making complex ideas easier to understand. Indeed, they can be good tools to explain
ideas to people outside your specialty. Some examples:

> *Dolby Stereo.* In the past decade the words "Dolby
> Stereo" have become familiar to music listeners and
> movie goers. I'm not an engineer, so I don't understand
> all of the bits and bytes of the Dolby process, but I once
> heard an engineer make the following metaphor for
> Dolby: "Dolby stereo is like a sonic laundry. It washes
> the dirt (or noise) out of the clothes (the signal) with-
> out disturbing the clothes (the signal)." I've asked other
> engineers about this, and they agree that Dolby is a
> "cleansing" process.

Personal Computers. Computer pioneer Steve Jobs once compared the personal computer to a bicycle in the following analogy:

> A few years ago, I read about the efficiency of locomotion for various species on the earth, including man. The study determined which species was the most efficient, in terms of getting from point A to point B with the least amount of energy exerted. The condor won. Man made a rather unimpressive showing about a third of the way down the list.
>
> But someone there had the insight to test a man riding a bicycle. Man was twice as efficient as the condor! This illustrated man's ability as a tool maker. When he created the bicycle, he created a tool that amplified an inherent ability. That's why I like to compare the personal computer to the bicycle. The personal computer is a 21st century bicycle if you will, because it's a tool that can amplify a certain part of our inherent intelligence. . . .

In a strict logical sense, a personal computer is *not* a bicycle, and Dolby is *not* a laundry. But by using such analogies, we enable ourselves to gain a new perspective on both the unfamiliar and the quite familiar.

Exercise: Make a metaphor for a problem you're currently dealing with or a concept you're developing. To do it, simply compare your concept to something else and then see what similarities you can find between the two ideas. Basically, you're using one idea to highlight another. See how far you can extend the comparison.

I've found that some of the most fertile (and easiest to develop) metaphors are those in which there is some action taking place. You might try comparing your concept to several or more of these:

Running for political office	Going on a diet
Disciplining a ten year old	Performing a magic trick
Cooking a fancy meal	Colonizing a territory
Running a marathon	Building a house
Starting a revolution	Spreading propaganda
Riding a roller coaster	Negotiating a contract
Prospecting for gold	Going fishing
Courting a woman	Planting a garden
Putting out a fire	Having a baby
Fighting a disease	Getting a divorce
Running a day care center	Arranging flowers
Sailing a ship in rough seas	Pruning a tree
Doing standup comedy	Conducting an orchestra
Attending a church service	Learning a new language

How is developing a new math curriculum like producing a television program? How is motivating a sales force like feeding the animals at a zoo? How is developing a marketing plan for a new baby product like camping in a wilderness area?

*   *   *

Our language is quite metaphorical, so much so that we don't realize it. There are clusters of metaphors that reflect what we think about various activities. One example is the metaphor used by some teachers who view their work as though they were horticulturalists. They talk about their students' basic ability to learn as the "seed" and their role is to provide the right "soil" and "sunlight" for their "growth." A student who is curious is spreading out his "roots." Some students are "potbound," while others "flower" and reach "fruition." Some students need a "hothouse" to develop, while others could prosper in a "desert."

Another example is the "Game of Life" metaphor in which business people use sports terminology to describe what they do. Everyone is trying to be "#1"; there are "management teams," "kickoff" meetings, and salespeople with "proven track records." You may "spar" with your manager, deal with "heavy-

weights" and "lightweights," and give a "knockout" performance.

My favorite example of this phenomenon is the language
used by financial people. Whenever I do any work with bank-
ers or accountants, they talk about what they do as though
they were plumbers. And no wonder! They use the "Water
Model of Finance" to describe their work.

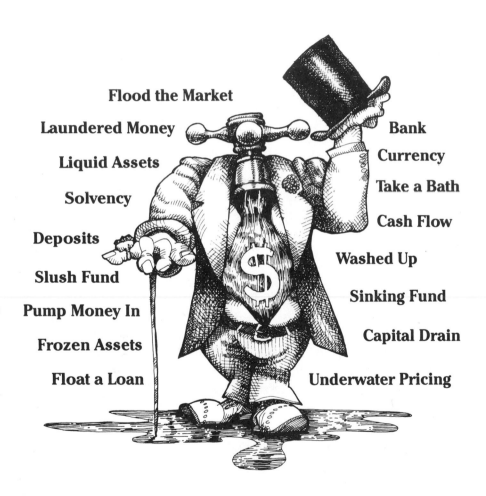

Flood the Market

Laundered Money   Bank

Liquid Assets   Currency

Solvency   Take a Bath

Deposits   Cash Flow

Slush Fund   Washed Up

Pump Money In   Sinking Fund

Frozen Assets   Capital Drain

Float a Loan   Underwater Pricing

Proverbs

Exercise: The Bible is quite metaphorical. Whether it's Jesus talking in parables or the prophets using similes to foretell the future, you'll find many ideas expressed metaphorically. This is particularly true in the Book of *Proverbs*. Here is a quiz from *Proverbs*. Connect the metaphor on the left side with the idea it represents on the right side.

Metaphor

1. A constant dripping on a rainy day (27:15)

2. A cool day in the hot summertime (25:13)

3. Chewing with a sore tooth (25:19)

4. A cloud blowing over the desert without dropping any rain (25:14)

5. A city with broken-down walls (25:28)

6. Yanking a dog's ears (26:17)

7. Sparks that fly when iron strikes iron (27:17)

8. Honey (16:24)

9. Polluting a stream (26:25)

10. A dog that returns to his vomit (26:11)

Its Reference

A. Kind words

B. A fool that repeats his folly

C. A faithful employee

D. Interferring in an argument that isn't your business

E. A stimulating friendly discussion

F. A good man who compromises with a wicked one

G. A man without self-control

H. A cranky woman

I. A person who doesn't give the gift he promised

J. Confiding in an unreliable person

The Meaning of Life

As you may have guessed by now, metaphors are one of my passions, and so I hope you'll excuse me for one more metaphorical indulgence.

One question I have is, "What is the meaning of life?" To find the answer, I have asked my seminar participants to make a metaphor for life. Their ideas can be put into two groups: those that deal with food, and those that don't. Here is the meaning of life:

Life is like a bagel. It's delicious when it's fresh and warm, but often it's just hard. The hole in the middle is its great mystery, and yet it wouldn't be a bagel without it.

Life is like eating grapefruit. First you have to break through the skin; then it takes a couple of bites to get used to the taste, and just as you begin to enjoy it, it squirts you in the eye.

Life is like a banana. You start out green and get soft and mushy with age. Some people want to be one of the bunch while others want to be top banana. You have to take care not to slip on externals. And, finally, you have to strip off the outer coating to get at the meat.

Life is like cooking. It all depends on what you add and how you mix it. Sometimes you follow the recipe and at other times, you're creative.

Life is like a jigsaw puzzle, but you don't have the picture on the front of the box to know what it's supposed to look like. Sometimes, you're not even sure if you have all the pieces.

Life is like a maze in which you try to avoid the exit.

Life is like riding an elevator. It has a lots of ups and downs and someone is always pushing your buttons. Sometimes you get the shaft, but what really bothers you are the jerks.

Life is like a poker game. You deal or are dealt to. It includes skill and luck. You bet, check, bluff, and raise. You learn from those you play with. Sometimes, you win with a pair or lose with a full house. But whatever happens, it's best to keep on shuffling along.

 Life is like a puppy dog always searching for a street full of fire hydrants.

 Life is like a room full of open doors that close as you get older.

What do you think life is like?

Summary

Logic is an important creative thinking tool. Its use is especially appropriate in the practical phase of the creative process when you are evaluating ideas and preparing them for action.

When you're searching for and playing with ideas, however, excessive logical thinking can short-circuit your creative process. That's because the imaginative phase is governed by a different logic that is best described as metaphorical, fantastic, elliptical, and ambiguous.

For more and better ideas, I prescribe a good dose of soft thinking in the imaginative phase of the creative process, and a hearty helping of hard thinking in the practical phase.

TIP: The metaphor is an excellent tool to help you "think something different." Think of yourself as a poet, and look for similarities around you. If you have a problem, make a metaphor. This should give you a fresh slant on it.

TIP: Go on metaphor hunts. Pay attention to the metaphors people use to describe what they are doing. For example, have you ever noticed how meteorologists use the "War Model of Weather" to describe their science?

TIP: Pay attention to the metaphors you use in your own thinking. As glorious a tool as metaphors are, they can easily imprison your thinking if you're not aware how much they're guiding your thoughts.

TIP: Remember, it's an illogical world. The glow worm isn't a worm. A firefly isn't a fly. The English horn isn't English (French) or a horn (woodwind). The Harlem Globetrotters didn't play a game in Harlem until they'd been playing for forty years. We name or refer to things not to be precise, but to grasp a sense of them.

3. Follow the Rules

Patterns: The Rules of the Game

Order is heav'n's first law.

—Alexander Pope, Poet

Let's suppose that you're watching television in your living room with some friends. Someone walks into the room, and as he does, he trips over a chair and knocks it down. This person picks up the chair and excuses himself for the commotion he's caused. What's your impression of this person? You probably think he's a klutz, right?

Okay, ten minutes later, another person walks into the room, and she too falls over the chair. Twenty minutes later, another person walks into the room, and the whole scene is repeated again. What is your opinion now? Probably that the chair is in the wrong place. Congratulations, you have recognized a pattern! You might even generalize this pattern into a rule such that anybody walking into the room will trip over the chair—unless, of course, the chair is moved.

Suppose I gave you the following series of numbers:

1, 4, 9, 16, 25, 36, 49

More than likely, you would quickly recognize a pattern, namely that each of the numbers is the square of its position in the series. You might feel so confident that you would predict that the next numbers in the series to be 64 and 81. Again, you have made a rule based on a pattern you have recognized.

What if you saw this list:

Painted Eggs
Fireworks
Champagne
Candy Canes
John Philip Sousa Music
Shamrocks
Jack-o'-Lanterns

At first, you probably wouldn't recognize much similarity between painted eggs and fireworks, but after reading through the rest of the list, you would realize that these things are all associated with American holidays. If we continued the list, you wouldn't be surprised to find egg nog, heart-shaped candy, the Unknown Soldier, ground hogs, and cherry trees.

With these three examples, we recognize another pattern, namely, that the human mind is very good at recognizing patterns. Indeed, I think that much of what we call "intelligence" is our ability to recognize patterns. We recognize sequences (the order in which you put on your clothes), cycles (pork prices and plankton yields conform to a strict four year boom-and-bust cycle), shapes (cracks in dried mud usually form 120° angles), processes (how to turn flour, eggs, and milk into waffles), similarities (stellar galaxies and water emptying in a bath tub spiral in the same way), and probabilities (the likelihood of throwing a "seven" at a crap table).

People see patterns everywhere—even when none is intended. A good example is the night sky. In fig. 1, we see a portion of the spring sky in the northern hemisphere.

Figure 1) A Portion of the Spring Sky

Looks like a bunch of stars, right? Well, thousands of years ago, the ancients looked up, emphasized some of the stars, made some connections, and came up with the figure of a lion—a celestial Rorschach!

Figure 2) The Constellation Leo

Patterns give us the power to understand the world, and as a consequence, they *rule* our thinking—they become the rules according to which we play the game of life.

Challenging the Rules

Every act of creation is first of all an act of destruction.
—Pablo Picasso, Artist

If constructing patterns were all that were necessary for creating new ideas, we'd all be creative geniuses. Creative thinking is not only *constructive,* it's also *destructive.* As we stated in the opening chapter, creative thinking involves playing with what you know, and this may mean breaking out of one pattern in order to create a new one. A very effective creative thinking strategy is to play the revolutionary and challenge the rules. Here's a good example.

In the winter of 333 B.C., the Macedonian general Alexander and his army arrive in the Asian city of Gordium to take up winter quarters. While there, Alexander hears about the legend surrounding the town's famous knot, the "Gordian Knot." A prophecy states that whoever is able to untie this strangely complicated knot will become king of Asia. This story intrigues

Alexander, and he asks to be taken to the knot so that he can attempt to untie it. He studies it for a bit, but after fruitless attempts to find the rope-ends, he is stymied.

"How can I unfasten the knot?" he asks himself. He gets an idea: "I'll just have to make up my own knot-untying rules" He pulls out his sword and slices the knot in half. Asia is fated to him.

With his postulation that the earth circles the sun, the Polish astonomer Copernicus broke the rule that that the universe is anthropocentric. With her evocative love odes, the Greek poet Sappho broke the rule that great lyric poetry was outside the province of women. With his use of trailing codas and double orchestral fugues, Beethoven broke the rules on how a symphony should be composed. With his lightning attacks of mechanized equipment, the German general Ernst Rommel broke the rules on how to fight a battle. With his equating mass and energy as different forms of the same phenomenon, Einstein broke the rules of Newtonian physics. Think about it: almost every advance in art, cooking, medicine, agriculture, engineering, marketing, politics, education, and design has occurred when someone challenged the rules and tried another approach.

Such rule-breaking happens in sports as well. Take swimming. Until the 1920's, there were only three competitive swimming strokes—freestyle, backstroke, and breaststroke—and each had specific rules that described how it was to be performed. The rules of breaststroke stated that both arms must be pulled together underwater and then recovered simultaneously back to the start of the pulling position to begin the next stroke. Most people interpreted this arm recovery to mean an *underwater* recovery. In the 1920's, however, someone challenged the rules and re-interpreted this arm recovery to be an *out-of-the-water* recovery. Since this new "breaststroke" was about 15% faster, people using the orthodox version couldn't effectively compete. Something had to be done. Finally, this new stroke—now known as the "butterfly"—won recognition as the fourth swimming stroke, and became an Olympic event in 1956. This has happened in other sports as well. If the rules hadn't been changed along the way, there would still be jump balls after every field goal in basketball; foul balls wouldn't count as strikes in baseball; and football wouldn't have a passing game.

I have a friend I go to whenever I have a really tough problem to solve. After I explain it to him, invariably his first question is, "What rules can we break?" He knows that I have assimilated so many rules into my thinking that after a while they become blind assumptions. It's difficult to be innovative if you're following blind assumptions.

The creative thinker is constantly challenging the rules. Most people will say, "As a rule, if operation 'XYZ' is done in a certain way, it will get these results 'alpha-beta-gamma.'" Here, "XYZ" can be a marketing strategy, a way to teach drawing to third graders, a choreography system, an engineering process, a fund-raising technique, or a way to stuff a turkey. The creative thinker will play with "XYZ" and look for results *outside* the usual rules and guidelines. One organization I know has gone so far as to incorporate this philosophy into their motto:

Every rule here can be challenged except this one.

They feel that if they are following the same rules five years from now, they won't have advanced the state of their art. They know that the rule that worked last year is probably valid this year, but they won't know for sure unless they challenge it.

Follow the Rules

If you don't ask "why this?" often enough, somebody will ask, "why you?"

—Tom Hirshfield, Physicist

Playing the revolutionary is easier said than done. One company president told me that his most difficult task is getting his subordinates to challenge the rules. He raises a good point. Why do people treat most problems and situations as closed ones with set rules, rather than as open ones that can be played with?

One main reason is that there is a lot of pressure in our culture to "follow the rules." This value is one of the first things we learn as children. We are told such things as: "No orange elephants," and "Don't color outside the lines." Our educational system encourages further rule-following. Students are usually better rewarded for regurgitating information than for playing with ideas and thinking originally. As a consequence, people feel more comfortable following the rules than challenging them.

From a practical standpoint, this value makes sense. In order to survive in society, you have to follow all kinds of rules. Shouting in a library, crying out "fire" in a packed theater, or cheating on your income taxes are three things *not* to do. If, however, you're trying to generate new ideas, then the value "follow the rules" can be a mental lock because it means: "think about things only as they are."

Warning: When I encourage you to challenge the rules, I'm not advocating you to do anything that's illegal, immoral, or unethical. Most of the rules you follow, however, aren't written down in some manual or book of legal statutes. In other words, they're unwritten rules such as the way you go to work, who cuts your hair, the type style you use most often, how your business forms are designed, what you say to other people in an elevator, or where you buy groceries. Unless you challenge them, you won't be more creative.

The Aslan Phenomenon

Creative thinking may simply mean the realization that there is no particular virtue in doing things the way they have always been done.

—Rudolph Flesch, Educator

Challenging the rules is a good creative thinking strategy, but that's not all. Never challenging the rules brings with it at least two potential dangers. The first is you can get locked into one approach, method, or strategy without seeing that other approaches might be more appropriate. As a result, you may tailor your problems to the preconceptions that enable you to solve them that way.

Another reason that the rules should be challenged is the "Aslan Phenomenon." It runs as follows:

1. We make rules based on reasons that make a lot of sense.

2. We follow these rules.

3. Time passes, and things change.

4. The original reasons for the generation of these rules may no longer exist, but because the rules are still in place, we continue to follow them.

For example, I like to run, and I have five or six routes that I'll take depending on how far I want to go. One of these is a route that goes through my neighborhood for about four miles. As a rule, the run ends about two blocks from our house, because several years ago, when I started this route, there was a big, friendly golden retriever living at the house where I stopped. His name was Aslan. After my run, I would take time to pet him, cool down, and steal his tennis ball. So stopping at Aslan's house became the rule for having a nice ending to a fun run.

But things have changed. His owner moved away and took Aslan with her. Nevertheless, whenever I take this route, I still stop at the same place—even though Aslan no longer lives there. There are probably more pleasurable places to end my run, but because I'm following an obsolete rule, I haven't looked for them.

Here's another example of the Aslan phenomenon. Take a look at the following configuration of letters:

Q W E R T Y U I O P

Are you familiar with them? You have undoubtedly seen this pattern many times. It is the top row of letters on a standardly configured typewriter or computer keyboard. It is known as the QWERTY configuration, and it has a fascinating history.

Back in the 1870's, Sholes & Co., a leading manufacturer of typewriters at the time, received many complaints from users about the typewriter keys sticking together if the operator went too fast. In response, management asked its engineers to figure out a way to prevent this from happening. The engineers discussed the problem for a bit and then one of them said, "What if we slowed the operator down? If we did that, the keys wouldn't jam together nearly as much." The result was to have an inefficient keyboard configuration. For example, the letters "O" and "I" are the third and sixth most frequently used letters in the English language, and yet the engineers positioned them on the key board so that the relatively weaker ring and little fingers had to depress them. This "inefficient logic" pervaded the keyboard, and this brilliant idea solved the problem of keyboard jam-up.

Since that solution, the state of the art in typewriter and word processing technology has advanced significantly. There are now typewriters and word processors that can go much faster than any human operator can type. The problem is that the QWERTY configuration continues to be used even though there are faster configurations available. Once a rule gets in place, it's very difficult to eliminate even though the original reason for its generation has disappeared. Thus, creative thinking involves not only generating new ideas, but escaping from obsolete ones as well.

NEW IDEA

OBSOLETE
IDEA

Not long ago I read about a group of Russian immigrants in Los Angeles who have the tradition of celebrating New Year's Eve on the afternoon of December 30th. A reporter for the Los Angeles *Times* heard about this and, thinking that there was a story there, went out to interview them. "Why are you celebrating the new year thirty-six hours before everyone else," she asked. One of them, a man in his late fifties responded, "When we were growing up in the Soviet Union forty years ago, we were very poor, and we found that it was a lot cheaper to get a band on December 30th. That's how the tradition started." The curious thing is that now most of these people are well off. They could easily afford lavish entertainment on New Year's Eve, and yet they still celebrate it on the previous afternoon. Almost every organization I've ever worked with—including my own—has some of the mentality of celebrating New Year's Eve early for some obsolete reason.

Slay A Sacred Cow

Sacred cows make great steaks.

—Richard Nicolosi, Businessman

Some rules are so successful that they become immune to criticism. These are the "sacred cows." As a result, people are afraid to challenge them. For example, it is said that Frederick the Great (1712-1786) lost the Battle of Jena which was fought in 1806. This means that for twenty years after his death, the army perpetuated his successful organization instead of adapting to meet the change in the art of war. Had his generals questioned Frederick's hallowed military tenets, they might have fared better against Napoleon.

Avoid falling in love with ideas. I got this advice from my printer. He said, "If you want to be successful, don't fall in love with a particular type style, because if you do, you'll want to use it everywhere—even in places where its inappropriate." I think that the same thing applies to ideas. I've seen people fall in love with a certain approach, and then be unable to see the merits of alternative approaches. I think that one of life's great thrills is falling out of love with a previously cherished idea. When that happens you're free to look for new ones.

Go after your sacred cows. Periodically inspect your ideas and beliefs to see if they are contributing to your thinking effectiveness. Ask yourself, "Why did this program, concept, project, or idea come to be?" Then follow this question with, "Do these reasons still exist?" If the answer is "no," then eliminate the idea. One person told me that he liked this link between elimination and innovation. He asked the eight people who worked with him to write down five things they didn't like about their jobs—ways of dealing with customers, paperwork, writing memos, policies, whatever. Curiously all eight people had three similar things on their lists. They focused on these, and were able to eliminate two of them as being obsolete.

Summary

Creative thinking is not only constructive, it's also destructive. Often, you have to break out of one pattern to discover another one.

Be flexible with the rules. Remember, breaking the rules won't necessarily lead to creative ideas, but it's one avenue. And staying on the same road may eventually lead to a dead end. After all, many rules outlive the purpose for which they were intended.

TIP: Play the revolutionary and challenge the rules—especially the ones you use to govern your day-to-day activities. If you usually start shaving on the left side of your face, tomorrow start on the right. If you never watch soap operas, watch some daytime television. If you usually listen to rock music, then listen to some jazz or classical music. If you usually work Monday through Friday, why not work the weekend and take the week off?

TIP: Remember that challenging the rules also has its dangers. One man told me that whenever he gets bored with a routine, he likes to throw what he calls a "perturbation" into the pattern to make it interesting. When he and his wife were in their mid-40's, they got bored with what they were doing and decided to have another child. Looking back on that decision, he said, "I think that we over-perturbated."

TIP: Have rule-inspecting and rule-discarding sessions within your organization. You may even find some motivational side benefits in this activity. Finding and eliminating outmoded rules can be a lot of fun. Perhaps Mark Twain had something like this in mind when he said, "One of life's most overvalued pleasures is sexual intercourse; and, one of life's least appreciated pleasure is defecation."

4. Be Practical

Exercise: Shown below is a design for a new chair. Write down three impressions you have about its value.

Design for a new chair

Exercise: What would happen if gravity stopped for one second every day? What would things be like? What would land surfaces look like? How about oceans and rivers? How would life have developed under such conditions? Would living things have special "zero-gravity" adaptive features? How would buildings and houses be designed? How about your furnishings?

Our Imaginative Seedbed

Human beings occupy a special niche in the order of things. Because we have the ability to symbolize our experience, our thinking is not limited to the real and the present. This capability empowers our thinking in two major ways. First, it enables us to anticipate the future. We're able to ask ourselves: "Suppose it rains tomorrow? What would happen to our picnic? What alternative arrangements should be made?" By simulating such possibilities in your mind, you can plan for the future.

Second, since our thinking is not bound by real world constraints, we can generate ideas that have no correlate in the world of experience. You did this in the exercise about gravity.

Similarly, you do it whenever you dream or imagine anything that doesn't actually exist.

I call the realm of the possible our "imaginative seedbed." There are a lot of good soft thinking tools for cultivating this seedbed. In this chapter, we'll focus on two of them: the "what if?" question and the "stepping stone."

What If?

Asking "what if?" is an easy but powerful way to get your imagination going. There are two simple steps involved.

Step #1: Simply ask "What if?" and then finish the question with some contrary-to-fact condition, idea, or situation.

Step #2: Answer the "what if" question.

The "what if" question can be whatever you wish. The nice thing about "what-iffing" is that it allows you to suspend a few assumptions, and get into an imaginative frame of mind. Some examples:

* What if animals became more intelligent than people?

* What if men also had babies?

* What if we elected our officials by lottery?

* What if we could make music by playing fruit and vegetables?

* What if people carried their homes and property on their backs like turtles?

* What if people had to marry people who were at least twenty years older or younger in age than they were?

* What if the price of a barrel of fresh water and a barrel of petroleum were the same?

* What if there were three sexes?

* What if when you looked in the mirror, there became two of you?

* What if highway "blacktop" came in "redtop" or "bluetop" depending on the speed limit?

* What if the airlines were able to load passengers on to planes as quickly as they unload them?

* What if people didn't need to sleep?

* What if human life-expectancy were 200 years?

✳ What if people had a set number of words each day they could speak on the telephone and if they exceeded that, the telephone police would come after them?

✳ What if people had to spend every third year living outside the country where they were born?

Now, let's ask and answer one:

What if we had seven fingers on each hand?

Would we be able to point and wave at the same time? Would we have two finger-opposing thumbs on each hand? If we did, would we have a better "grasp" on things? You could name your fingers after the days of the week, and if you didn't like something you could flip that person a "Wednesday." If you were clumsy, you could say, "Sorry, I'm all weekends."

How would seven fingers on each hand affect sports? How would we catch balls? Would we become more sure–handed? Can't you just see some players, after a good play, saying: "Gimme seven, gimme fourteen." That raises an interesting point: maybe our number system would be base 14 instead of base 10.

Would more people be in the jewelry business? What kind of piano music would be written? What would hand tools look like? How about typewriter and computer keyboards. How would they be arranged? Would there be more shift keys? Maybe instead of a keyboard there would be "keyspheres"–balls with keys on them that you squeezed to get the letters you wanted.

At the very least, this question makes us think about something we take very much for granted—our fingers.

Let's take a look at another "what if." Here is one person's view of what would happen if we lived our lives backwards.

Life is tough. It takes up a lot of your time, all your weekends, and what do you get at the end of it? Death, a great reward.

The life cycle is all backwards. You should die first, and get it out of the way. Then you live for twenty years in an old age home, and get kicked out when you're too young. You get a gold watch and then you go to work. You work forty years until you're young enough to enjoy your retirement.

You go to college and you party until you're ready for high school. Then you go to grade school, you become a little kid, you play, you have no responsibilities, you become a little baby, you go back into the womb, you spend your last nine months floating, and you finish off as a gleam in somebody's eye.

You can see that asking "what if?" questions is not only a lot of fun, it also gives you the freedom to think along different lines.

Who should whack himself with this soft thinking tool? Everybody—housewives, salespeople, children, teachers, comedians, doctors, florists, managers, and you—can all benefit from asking "what if?" It's a way of freeing yourself from the deeply ingrained assumptions you have about your work and your personal life. I've known designers who would ask themselves such questions as: "What if we made our products uglier and less reliable?" I've known engineers who tried to imagine "how something would function without one of its main parts" just to see what would happen.

The real key to asking "what if" is allowing yourself to probe the possible, the impossible, and even the impractical for ideas. Here are two specific "what if" strategies for you to try.

Imagine How Others Would Do It

A good way to stretch your imagination is to ask "what if" someone else were solving your problem. How would this person—for example, Winston Churchill, Machiavelli, your mother, George Patton, Mother Teresa, the Three Stooges, the Godfather, Jesus of Nazareth, Wonder Woman, Sigmund Freud, Arturo Toscanini, Martin Luther King, or a seven year old girl— go about it? What assumptions would they bring in? What constraints would they ignore? What special twists would they give to it? What special expertise would they add? What innovative changes would they make?

For example, let's suppose that you're the principal of a high school. What if someone with a mindset like Walt Disney had your job? How would he approach it? What things would change? For one thing, there might be more emphasis on graphics and visual learning. Students would learn through experience, e.g., they might study the Civil War by making scenes of different battles. They would learn history by pretending they were the characters they were studying. Imagine the playground: students would learn physics, engineering, and chemistry from building rides for the school. There might be more field trips. The motto would be "Being open-minded is the key to education" or "If you don't take risks, you won't achieve what you want." Students would enjoy school more, thus boosting attendance. And there would be a greater emphasis on students' learning creativity skills.

Whom do you respect for creative achievement? A leader in your field? A teacher? A parent? Now imagine that one of these is responsible for developing your concept. What would they do? How would they approach it? What innovative changes would they make?

Imagine You're the Idea

Another "what if?" technique is to imagine that you are the concept you're trying to develop. For example, suppose you're trying to improve the design of a toaster. What would it would be like to actually be a toaster? How would you receive bread? What would it be like when your heating elements go on? What happens when caraway seeds fall to the bottom? What would it be like to cool down?

Imagine that you're a box of cereal on a grocery shelf. How can you be more attractive? How can you stand out from the other brands? What can you do to force the grocer to give you more shelf space?

What if you are working to change the design of a parking meter? Now, imagine what it's like to be a parking meter.

How does it feel when coins are inserted in you? What does it feel like when you have "expired." How could you be easier to use? What would you look like if you took credit cards? How would the magnetic strip feel?

The results of such playful speculation can yield quite practical results. A noted scientist once asked himself, "What if I were an elevator falling through space at the speed of light. What if there was a hole in the side of the elevator? What if a shaft of light came through this hole into the elevator? What would happen? What would the light's behavior be?" By investigating the ramifications of such a possibility, Albert Einstein developed some of his early relativity concepts.

I have a friend whom I talk with about the creative process. She thinks that my ideas are interesting but that "what really happens in the inner chamber of creative thought is indistinguishable from magic." She makes a good point. Our thinking is quite magical. Try playing the magician—the person who specializes in asking the fantasy "what if" question.

If you take any activity, any art, any discipline, any skill, take it and push it as far as it will go, push it beyond where it has ever been before, push it to the wildest edge of edges, then you force it into the realm of magic.

—Tom Robbins, Author

The Stepping Stone

"What if" questions, by themselves, may not produce practical, creative ideas. Thus, it may be necessary to use another thinking tool—the stepping stone. Stepping stones are simply provocative ideas that stimulate us to think about other ideas. Stepping stones may be impractical or improbable, but their value consists not in how practical they are, but in where they lead your thinking. Remember, when you are in the imaginative phase, real world constraints do not apply. It often happens that an impractical idea leads to a practical, creative one. The following story is a good example of this phenomenon.

Several years ago, an engineer at a large chemical company asked the following question: "What if we put gunpowder in our house paint?" The people around him were somewhat taken aback, but the engineer continued.

Have you ever noticed what happens to paint after it's been on a house for five or six years? It chips and cracks and is very difficult to remove. There has to be a better way to get it off. If we put gunpowder in our house paint, we could just blow it right off the house.

The engineer had an interesting idea, but it had one drawback—it wasn't very practical. The people who were listening to this man, however, did something very much to their credit. They didn't evaluate his idea on the basis of its practical merits. On the contrary, they approached it as a stepping stone which might lead them to a practical, creative solution. They thought, "What other ways are there to create a chemical reaction that would remove the old house paint?" This question opened up their thinking and eventually lead to the idea of putting additives in their house paint. These additives would be inert until another solution containing other additives was applied to the old paint at a later date. At this point, a reaction would take place between the two sets of additives that would cause the paint to strip right off. That company went on to make such a process a reality.

A few years ago, a city in the Netherlands had a refuse problem. A once-clean section of town had become an eye-sore because people had stopped using the trash cans. There were cigarette butts, beer bottles, chocolate wrappers, newspapers, and other trash littering the streets.

Obviously, the sanitation department was concerned, so they sought ways to clean up the city. One idea was to double the littering fine from 25 guilders to 50 guilders for each offense. They tried this, but it had little effect. Another approach was to increase the number of litter-agents who patrolled the area. This was more of the same, that is, another "punish the litterer" solution, and it, too, had little impact on the problem. Then somebody asked the following question:

> What if our trash cans paid people money when they put their trash in? We could put an electronic sensing devise on each can as well as a coin-return mechanism. Whenever a person put trash in the can, it would pay him 10 guilders.

This idea, to say the least, whacked everyone's thinking. The what-iffer had changed the situation from a "punish the litterer" problem to a "reward the law abider" problem. The idea had one glaring fault, however; if the city implemented the idea, it would go bankrupt. Half of Europe would come to use their trash cans.

Fortunately, the people who were listening to this idea didn't evaluate it based on its practical merits. Instead, they used it as a stepping stone and asked themselves: "What other ways are there in which we can reward people for putting their refuse in the trash cans?" This question lead to the following solution. The sanitation department developed electronic trash cans which had a sensing unit on the top that would detect when a piece of refuse had been deposited. This would activate a tape recorder that would play a recording of a joke. In other words, joke-telling trash cans! Different trash cans told different kinds of jokes (some told bad puns while others told shaggy dog stories and still others told snappy one-liners) and soon developed reputations. The jokes were changed every two weeks. As a result, people went out of their way to put their trash in the trash cans, and the town became clean once again. (For those of you who are interested, that is the origin of the comedy term "throw-away" line.)

Here's another example. A group of researchers at a dog food company asked:

> What if we put non-digestible additives—for example, flower seeds—in our products? Dogs would then become delivery systems going about planting and fertilizing flowers in the neighborhood. Another additive might be a non-toxic fluorescent material. This would be especially appropriate in cities at night where pedestrians would know that the glowing object up ahead is something they don't want to step on.

This discussion didn't lead to any new dog food products, but it did lead to several practical cattle feed ideas. One is a way of putting grass seed in cattle feed as a way of re-seeding range lands. Another is creating a fluorescent salt lick. Wild life rangers could then more closely monitor targeted animals. A third is a "pesticide" (non-toxic and non-digestible) that harmlessly passes through the cow to become part of the cow feces. Certain disease-breeding flies that are attracted to the feces are eliminated by their contact with it.

The point is this: you don't execute stepping stones, you launch your thinking from them. Indeed, there are some creative ideas that can only be reached by going through a stepping stone or two.

Be Practical

The human mind likes a strange idea as little as the body likes a strange protein and resists it with a similar energy.
—W.I. Beveridge, Scientist

Why don't people use "what if" thinking and stepping stones more often to generate ideas? There are three main reasons. The first is that when people look at new ideas, they tend to be critical and focus in on what's out of whack. For example, what were your comments about the new chair design at the beginning of this chapter? If you're like a lot of people, you probably said something like:

> ▼ "It looks uncomfortable."

> ▼ "It's impractical. It would fall over as soon as some-one tried to sit on it."

> ▼ "It's ugly."

Notice that all of the comments are negative. Many people don't ask where the chair is going to be used or what the purpose is. What if it were to be used on the moon or underwater? Would that change your assessment?

In addition to finding out what's wrong with a new idea, it's important to focus in on what's worth building on. Sometimes a drawback can serve as a stepping stone to a practical, creative idea. For example:

> ▲ "Perhaps the blade is retractable; when you want to keep your shedding dog or cat off the chair, have the blade up. When you want to sit down, retract it."

> ▲ "Meetings would be shorter and to the point."

> ▲ "It's a good chair for three o'clock in the after-noon when everyone's sleepy."

Here's an evaluation tip. When you judge new ideas, focus initially on their positive, interesting, and potentially useful features. Ask yourself: what needed function will this perform? This approach will not only counteract a natural negative bias, it will also enable you to develop more ideas. For example: what are five benefits to sleeping in your clothes?

A second reason that we don't ask "what if" more often is that this tool is low-probability in character. It's fairly unlikely that any particular "what if" question will produce a practical, creative idea. Thus, you may have to ask many "what if" questions and follow out many stepping stones before reaching a practical, creative idea. How many "what if" questions did Einstein ask himself before he boarded his imaginary elevator? A hundred? Two hundred? No matter. He eventually got a good idea which he probably wouldn't have gotten had he stayed in the practical realm. Thus, even though the likelihood of any given "what if" question reaching fruition is low, a few imaginative ideas will bear fruit in the world of action. Most people, however, don't feel they have the time to do this, so they limit themselves to the more practical "what is."

The third reason we don't use these tools is that we haven't been taught to. What happens to our imaginations as we mature? When we are young, they are cultivated in fairy tales and imagination games, but then we are told to "grow up." As people grow older, they get used to the "what is" of reality and forget about the possibilities that asking "what if" can generate. One of my workshop participants had this appraisal:

The amount a person uses her imagination is inversely proportional to the amount of punishment she will receive for using it.

Her implication: it's okay for children but not for adults to spend their time "what-iffing." We have been trained to respond to the unusual by saying, "That's not practical," instead of, "Hey, that's interesting; I wonder where that will lead our thinking." If the people who were discussing "gunpowder paint" or "coin-return trash cans" had said, "be practical," they never would have given themselves an opportunity to take a imaginative idea and turn it into a usable one. As Picasso put it:

Every child is an artist. The problem is how to remain an artist after growing up.

To be sure, you need to be practical for almost all of your daily activities. If you aren't, you probably won't survive very long. You can't live on imaginary food, or stop your car with "what if brakes" that save brake lining by working only 75% of the time. Being practical is important in the world of action, but practicality alone will not generate new ideas. The logic that works so well in judging and executing ideas may stifle the creative process if it prevents the artist in you from exploring unusual imaginative ideas.

Summary

This world was built by practical people who knew how to get into an imaginative frame of mind, listen to their imaginations, and build on the ideas they found there.

TIP: Each of you has an "artist" and a "judge" within you. The open-minded attitude of the artist typifies the kind of thinking you use in the imaginative phase when you're generating ideas. The evaluative outlook of the judge represents the kind of thinking you use in the practical phase when you're preparing ideas for execution. I recommend that you avoid bringing in your judge before your artist has had a chance to do her job. Premature evaluation can prevent conception.

TIP: Cultivate your imagination. Set aside time every day to ask yourself "what if" questions. Use the provocative answers you find as stepping stones to new ideas. Although the likelihood that any given "what if" question will lead to a practical idea isn't high, the more often you practice this activity, the more productive you'll become.

TIP: Encourage "what-iffing" in others. Many of my clients have established a "what if" question of the week within their departments as a way of looking for potential problems and opportunities. "What if the cost of money doubled in the next six months?" "What if the market for our largest-selling product shrank to 25% its current size?" "What if we only went to work three days a week and did the rest of the work at home?" "What if students went to school seven days a week twelve months a year?"

TIP: The playwright Jerome Lawrence has an evaluation technique, the "creative no," that he uses whenever he's collaborating with someone else. It works like this: either member of the partnership can veto the other's ideas. However, when one partner does exercise this veto, he also takes responsibility for coming up with a new idea that both partners like. Thus, it's not only destructive, it's constructive as well.

5. Play Is Frivolous

The Moment of Conception

Exercise: During what kinds of activities and situations do you get your ideas? For example, doing routine work, as a response to questions, during physical exercise, late at night, driving, in the company of others, etc.

I've asked this question to hundreds of thousands of people. The answers I've received can be grouped into two categories. The first is "necessity," and it is represented by replies such as:

> "When I'm faced with a problem."

> "When things break down, and I have to fix them."

> "When there's a need to be filled."

> "When the deadline is near . . . that's the ultimate inspiration."

These responses bear out the old adage that "necessity is the mother of invention." But interestingly enough, an equal if not greater number of people get their ideas in the opposite situation, and they respond along these lines:

> "When I'm just playing around."

> "When I'm doing something else."

> "When I'm not taking myself too seriously."

> "After my second beer."

From this I conclude that necessity may be the mother of invention, but play is certainly the *father.* As we said in the opening chapter, a playful attitude is fundamental to creative thinking. I'll bet that you generate most of your new ideas when you're playing in your mental playground. That's because your defenses are down, your mental locks are loosened, and there is little concern with the rules, practicality, or being wrong. When you play, you give yourself an invitation to reinvent reality and to reformulate established ways of doing things. Most of life presents you with a win/lose proposition: if you don't win, you lose. This is true for most games, sports, elections, coin-tosses, bets, arguments, and the like. When you play, however, a different logic is at work: a win/no-win logic. This is an important difference because it means that instead of being penalized for our mistakes, we learn from them. Thus, when we win, we win. When we don't, we learn. This is a nice arrangement. The only thing it costs is the time to do it.

Children know that play is a good way to learn. Take a look at kids kicking a soccer ball. They'll pass it around, play all sorts of games with it, and most important, they'll improve their soccer skills. Watch children play with a computer. They experiment and try all kinds of approaches. Pretty soon, they are proficient. One reason children are so good at play is that they don't know all of the "supposed to's."

Some people, however, think that if you're just playing at something, then you're really not working on it. Their attitude is, "Stop playing games and get down to business." They view work and play as two mutually exclusive boxes, and if you aren't producing hard tangible results, then you aren't working. They feel, in other words, that "play is frivolous."

A computer architect I know has this to say about play:

Play is what I do for a living. The work comes in organizing the results of the play.

He realizes that there are two sides to the creative process. The play side enables him to try various approaches in order to learn what works and what doesn't and to take this knowledge to germinate new ideas. The work side enables him to take what he has learned, evaluate it, corroborate it with existing knowledge, and to put it into a useful form.

Some of the most important inventions and ideas were originally conceived for the purpose of play—their practical value to be discovered later. A good example of this is the Moebius strip, a one-sided surface that has many unexpected properties. This topological idea was discovered by the German mathematician and astronomer Augustus Ferdinand Moebius.

You can make a Moebius strip by taking a strip of paper and making a loop out of it. But before connecting the two ends, give one of them a half-twist. This loop now only has one side. You can prove this to yourself by taking a pencil and drawing a line all the way around the loop. Soon you will come back to your starting point. You will have covered the entire loop, thus proving that it has only one side. (It also has only one edge!)

Now take a pair of scissors and cut the strip along the line you have just drawn. What happens? Most loops, when cut in half, form two smaller loops. But this isn't so with the Moebius strip—it becomes one loop twice as long (but now it has two sides and is no longer a Moebius strip). Now try cutting a Moebius strip into thirds. This produces another surprise: two intertwined loops, one a two-sided loop and the other a Moebius strip.

For years, the Moebius strip was considered to be the "plaything of topology"—a nice amusement but not much more. In the last forty years, however, some practical applications have been found for the Moebius strip. Rubber manufacturers have used the Moebius strip for conveyor belts. The belt lasts longer because both sides are actually one and receive equal wear. Electronic engineers have found that a resistor with a twist bent back on itself performs its function more efficiently. A continuous loop in a cassette cartridge will play twice as long if it has a twist in it. Chemists are exploring ways of making molecules in the shape of the Moebius strip. When they split, the get bigger rather than smaller.

Laugh At It

As soon as you have made a thought, laugh at it.

—Lao Tzu, Philosopher

An important form of play is humor. I believe that if you can laugh at something—be it a problem, a project, a recipe for chicken, how airplanes are designed, or your relationship with another person—then you're more likely to think about it in a fresh way. Laughter puts you at ease. Do you feel more comfortable talking with someone who has just told you a joke, or with someone who is deadly serious? Would you rather listen to a speaker who approaches his subject in a plodding straightforward manner or one who has just given you a humorous aside on the state of your business?

Getting into a humorous frame of mind not only loosens you up, it enhances your creativity. This has been demonstrated in studies investigating the role humor plays in stimulating a creative outlook. Typically the tests are run as follows: test participants are divided into two equal groups. One group sits silently in a study hall for a half an hour prior to the test. The other group spends the same time in another room listening to an audio tape of a standup comedian telling jokes like:

Question: How deep is the ocean?

Answer: Just a stone's throw.

Question: What do John the Baptist and Winnie the Pooh have in common?

Answer: They both have the same middle name.

Question: What do you get when you combine the Godfather with a lawyer?

Answer: An offer you can't understand.

Then both groups take the creativity test. The group that's involved in the comedy usually does much better. The comedy loosens up their thinking and establishes an environment in which people can be creative.

Why is this? First, humor stretches your thinking. The term "just a stone's throw" typically denotes a short distance. But when you throw a rock into water, it travels until it reaches the bottom—perhaps as much as seven miles depending on where you toss it. The punch line forces you to make a shift in how you think about a "stone's throw." Getting the joke then is an exercise in "breaking set"—one of the key aspects of "thinking something different." For if a stone's throw can mean *seven miles,* who is to stop you from looking at a broken light bulb as a *knife,* a vacuum cleaner as a *musical instrument,* snails as *food,* a clothespin as a *toy,* or a box of packaged baking soda as *refrigerator deodorant?*

Secondly, humor forces you to combine ideas that are usually not associated with one another. Few people think of "John the Baptist" and "Winnie the Pooh" as having much in common. The former was a first century Jewish prophet who baptized Jesus; the latter a frivolous fictional bear created nineteen centuries later by the English poet A.A. Milne. Yet for purposes of this joke, this unlikely pair is brought together. In a world where John the Baptist and Winnie the Pooh can be thrown together into one concept, what's to stop you from combining television sets and flea repellent into one idea? Or sunglasses and prayer meetings? Or freeway congestion and bookmarks? If you think hard enough, you'll think of a connection. This type of thinking is also at the core of creativity. The ancients combined soft iron with even softer tin to create hard bronze. The first person to put a satellite dish on the back of a truck to create a mobile uplink-downlink station did this. So did the person who combined a surfboard and a sail to create the sport of windsurfing. So did the person who combined movies and airplanes to create in-flight entertainment. I'm sure you can think of many other creations that were the combination of simple ideas.

Third, humor allows you to take things less seriously. In the Godfather-lawyer joke, both attorneys and Mafia Dons are targeted. Just how effective would a Godfather be if he couldn't threaten people? How effective would an attorney be if he couldn't find and create loopholes? If you can make fun of something, then you're more likely to challenge the rules that give that "something" its legitimacy, and perhaps you can think of alternatives.

This is not meant to be a treatise on humor. (Heaven knows! Some of the most boring works around are those describing humor.) But the point is this: there is a close relationship between the "haha" of humor and the "aha!" of discovery. If you employ the same thinking that you use in humor—break-

ing set, putting ideas into different new contexts, seeking ambiguity, combining different ideas, asking unusual "what if" questions, parodying the rules—and apply it to problem-solving,
then you're likely to come up with some fresh approaches to
what you're working on.

Humor may not solve your problem, but it will put you in a
more conducive mood to do so. From my own experience con-
ducting creativity workshops, I've found that humor works
wonders to stimulate the flow of ideas. If early on in a session I
encourage the participants to be humorous in their approach
to the problem, their answers are usually much more interesting and provocative. Not only that, they're more candid in their
approach to the more serious issues that I subsequently present to them. The corollary of this is that if I don't use humor
early on, the people are likely to sit on their hands and be judg-
mental.

Here's my advice:

Go ahead and be whacky.
Get into a crazy frame of mind
and ask what's funny about
what you're doing.

Humor is an effective tool even with the gravest of problems. As the physicist Niels Bohr once put it, "There are some
things that are so serious that you have you laugh at them."
Some people are so closely married to their ideas that they put
them up on a pedestal. It's difficult to be creative when you
have that much ego tied up in your idea. Therefore, step back,
loosen up, and remember Laroff's credo:

It's not so important to be serious as
it is to be serious about the important
things. The monkey wears an express-
ion of seriousness that would do credit
to any great scholar. But the monkey
is serious because he itches.

Have Fun

One of play's products is fun—one of the most powerful motivators around. I've noticed that a fun working environment is significantly more productive than a routine environment. People who enjoy what they do will come up with more ideas. The fun is contagious, and everybody works harder to get a piece of it.

One woman told me that one of her keys to success is playfulness. "Whenever we hire new people, we're not so concerned with how intelligent or efficient they are. To me, the important characteristics are their playfulness and intensity. When people have these two traits, they're enthusiastic—and these are the ones who generate new ideas." (Note: the Greek word *enthousiasmos* means "the God within you." Enthusiastic people seem to have access to a spirit which serves as their source of inspiration.)

Exercise: Suppose someone in your organization put the following announcement on the bulletin board:

ATTENTION!

John Roe is now the proud papa of a bouncing 8 lb. 3 oz. baby boy! Mama and baby are doing fine and resting comfortably at St. Joe's.

What would you think if you saw this?

Well, one person I know had this happen to him, and as soon as he saw this he heard the "knock of opportunity." He worked for an engineering group that had been under a lot of pressure, and he was looking for ways to make the working environment more fun. He felt that this was a chance for people to exercise their creativity. And so, underneath the birth announcement he wrote:

Name the Baby Contest!

For the next two days, his colleagues posted their ideas on the bulletin board. Here are some of the names that were submitted:

Zor Roe	Merrill Lynmon Roe
Henry David Thor Roe	Yermy Hee Roe
Scissor Roe	Meist Roe
A Long Hoadto Roe	Skid Roe
Phar Roe	Beg Steelerbar Roe
Wis Key Roe	Agnew Spear Roe
Wheel Bar Roe	Getcher Ducksina Roe
Kye Roe	Clarence Dar Roe
Fidel Cast Roe	Broken Air Roe
Edin Bur Roe	Bone Mare Roe
Jeth Roe	Kilimanja Roe
A Tennisp Roe	Sagua Roe
Figer Roe	Maha Gony Roe
Edward Armour Roe	Mike Roe
Af Roe	Velk Roe

Marymaryquitecontraryhowdoesyourgarden G. Roe
Withsilverbellscockleshellsandprettymaidsallina Roe

Can you think of some other possibilities?

Everyone had a lot of fun with this and it got their creative juices going. And it made their work environment more fun, which was what my friend was seeking.

Twelve-Sided Fun

Everyone has a favorite mathematical idea. Mine is the twelve-sided geometrical solid, the dodecahedron. (It's one of only five regular solids—the others being the tetrahedron, the cube, the octohedron, and the icosahedron.) Believe it or not, many of the ideas in this book were generated while I was constructing and playing with dodecahedra.

You can make your very own dodecahedron by copying the template on the next page on to a thick piece of paper or cardboard. Cut along the solid lines and fold along the dotted lines. Fold each triangular tab under the adjacent pentagon and tape (or glue) down. After awhile, you'll have your own dodecahedron to play with. You might even think of various things to put on the different sides.

Since this book was first published, I have received a variety of different dodecahedron applications. One person turned it into a Christmas card celebrating the twelve days of Christmas which the recipient could then fold into a Christmas tree ornament. Another person put twelve different shaped doodles on it to stimulate her thinking. Still another person started a company that produces dodecahedra with advice for solving specific problems printed on the different faces.

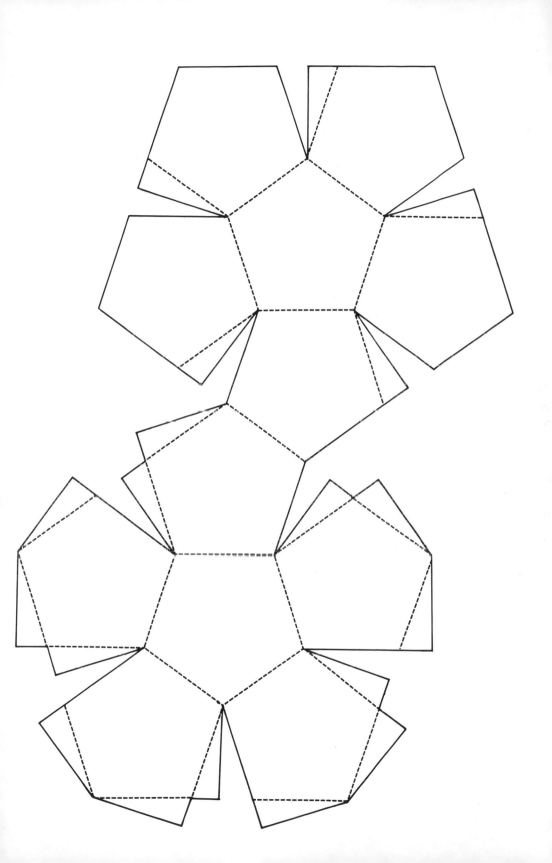

Summary

If necessity is the mother of invention, play is the father. Use it to fertilize your thinking.

TIP: The next time you have a problem, play with it.

TIP: If you don't have a problem, take time to play anyway. You may find some new ideas.

TIP: Make your work place a fun place to be.

TIP: Laugh at yourself. What's the funniest thing you've done in the last year? What did you learn?

6.That's Not My Area

The Solar Cell

A solar energy lab technician has a problem. Her research lab is experimenting with a new solar cell material, gallium arsenide, which is causing her problems in the slicing stage of cell production. Her task is to use a special high-speed wafer saw to make precision cuts in the material. But every time she cuts the material it cracks. She tries changing the position of the saw. The material still cracks. She is quite frustrated.

At home that weekend, she is in her husband's shop watching him make cabinets. She notices that when he wants to make precision cuts on certain types of wood, he reduces (rather than increases) the saw's cutting speed. She gets an idea: why not try the same approach on the gallium arsenide. She does, and it works.

What this woman did exemplifies an important part of creative thinking: recognizing the basic idea of one situation and applying it to another. The benefits of transferring knowledge gained in one area to another seem obvious. Why don't people do it more often?

One answer is specialization. As a strategy for managing information, specialization is essential. There is so much going on that it's impossible to pay attention to everything. Each second our nervous system is bombarded by approximately 100,00 bits of information. If we responded to that much information, our nervous systems would snap. It would be like a clam trying to siphon up all the sludge in San Francisco Bay–it just can't be done. Thus, one benefit of specialization is that it allows us to reduce the amount of irrelevant and trivial outside information we take in.

Similarly, as a strategy for getting along in the world, specialization is a necessity. In order to be effective in most endeavors–education, business, sports, technology, cooking– you have to narrow your area and become an expert. Look at baseball. It used to be that relief pitchers were used sparingly; the starters were expected to go all the way. Now there is a whole array of specialized relievers: long relievers, intermediate relievers, short relievers, relievers who throw smoke to right-handed batters, etc. Look at the variety of different types of accountants: tax specialists, management specialists, estate planning specialists, audit specialists, and so on.

The more complicated things become, the higher the walls go between the specialties. When I was in graduate school, I knew a marine biologist who was unable to talk with a molecular biologist because of the specialized nature of their disciplines. So, we have a situation where people know more and more about less and less.

That's Not My Area

As a strategy for creative thinking, specialization is dangerous because it can lead to the attitude "that's not my area." When this happens, a person may not only delimit her problems to too small an area, she may also stop looking for ideas in other fields.

How many times have you heard someone say, "That's an administration problem," "That's a marketing problem," or "That's an engineering problem"? We hear it all the time. Very few problems, however, are pure engineering problems. Most are engineering and manufacturing problems—and perhaps even marketing problems. Most data processing problems are not only DP problems, but also communications and finance problems. But if a person thinks, "that's not my area," she won't be defining the problem in such broad terms.

Here is an example of some of the consequences of this attitude. One of my manufacturing clients had a "single-sourced" capacitor designed into a circuit-board his company was producing. Manufacturing people typically go out of their way to avoid single-sourced parts, i.e., those produced by only one outside vendor. They reason that if only one vendor is producing a particular sub-component, then an entire manufacturing group can be idled if anything happens to the vendor's capability to produce.

Things were fine until the vendor had production problems

and could no longer meet demand. My client spent a lot of time attempting to track down more capacitors, but was unsuccessful. Finally, he went back through five layers of management to the design department to see how critical this capacitor was, and if it would be possible to use a replacement. When the design engineer was asked why this particular capacitor had been chosen, he replied, "I chose it because it's blue, and it looks good on the circuit board." The designer had never bothered to consider what impact such a choice would actually have on getting the product out the door. His tunnelvision had prevented him from even looking for such a problem.

This happens in other professions as well. One of my brothers-in-law is a physician. He has told me that he has noticed a tendency on the part of some doctors to look at their patients from the point of view of their specialties. For example, the orthopedic surgeons with this attitude don't look at their patients as people, but as a set of bones; the cardiologists look at their patients as sick or healthy hearts, and so on. Thus, they overlook the role the mind plays in healing. As a reaction to this, we are seeing the rise of holistic medicine and the wellness movement.

Cross-Fertilization

I have worked with the movie and television industries, the advertising profession, high technology research groups, packaged goods groups, hospital and health care professionals, and art departments. The one common denominator I have found is that each culture feels that it is the most creative, and that its members have a special elixir for new ideas. I think this is nice. *Esprit de corps* helps to create a good working environment. But I also feel that television people could learn a lot from elementary school teachers, and that research and development could pick up a few ideas from advertising. Every culture, industry, discipline, department, and organization has its own metaphors, models, methodologies, and short cuts for dealing with problems. But often the best ideas come from cutting across disciplinary boundaries and looking into other fields for new ideas. Many significant advances in art, business, education, entertainment, politics, and science have come about through a cross-fertilization of ideas. And to give a corollary, nothing will make a field stagnate more quickly than keeping out foreign ideas.

Here are a few examples of how people have taken ideas from one field and used them to make discoveries in another:

◆ An aerospace manager told me that he took up the hobby of designing and constructing backyard water-falls for himself and his friends. "I don't know why," he said, "but designing waterfalls has made me a better manager. It has brought me a lot closer in touch with concepts such as *flow, movement,* and *vibration.* These concepts are difficult to put into words, but they are important in communicating between two people."

◆ I recently read about a birth control device developed by a gynecologist collaborating with a dentist. An usual combination! We'd expect the gynecologist–who else specializes in female anatomy? But the dentist? The dentist, however, makes much of his living working with forms, shapes, and molds.

◆ The real estate entrepreneur Frank Morrow explains that he got his entrepreneurial education while attending the Graduate School of Business at Stanford–but not in the usual way. "I took all of the required courses in marketing, finance, accounting, and so on, but I learned more about business from a drawing course taught by the artist Nathan Olivera. What Olivera taught was: 'All art is a series of recoveries from the first line. The hardest thing to do is to put down the first line. But you must.' The same is true in business. You must act. A lot of business school types analyze things to death and never get around to acting. Perhaps more of them should take drawing courses."

◆ I once asked computer entrepreneur Steve Jobs why some people are more creative than others. He replied, "Innovation is usually the result of connections of past experience. But if you have the same experiences as everybody else, you're unlikely to look in a different direction. For example, I went to Reed College in Portland. At Reed, most of the men took modern dance classes from a woman named Judy Massey. We did it to meet the women. I didn't realize how much I learned about movement and perception from that class until a few years later when I worked for Nolan Bushnell at Atari. I was able to relate how much resolution of movement you need in terms of perceiving things in certain ways for video games."

Exercise: "Most advances in science," explains physicist Peter Borden, "come when a person is forced to change fields." You can "change fields" briefly by taking someone to lunch. Let's suppose that the following pairs of people went to lunch together. What could they learn from one another?

➡ A bus driver and a comedian.

➡ A beautician and an insurance salesman.

➡ An automobile mechanic and a politician.

➡ A kindergarten teacher and a software programmer.

➡ A priest and the head waiter at a fancy restaurant.

➡ A nurse in a cancer ward and a jazz drummer.

➡ An airline pilot and a geologist.

➡ A choreographer and a bookie.

➡ A prostitute and a professional football player.

➡ A policeman and a librarian.

➡ A circus clown and an air traffic controller.

➡ A bull fighter and a gardener.

➡ A fool and a banker.

Be An Explorer

Anyone can look for fashion in a boutique
or history in a museum. The creative
person looks for history in a hardware
store and fashion in an airport.

–Robert Wieder, Journalist

It's one thing to be open to new ideas; it's quite another to
go on the offensive and actively seek them out. I encourage you
to be a "explorer" and search for ideas outside your area. A
good explorer knows that looking for good ideas is like pros-
pecting for gold. If you look in the same old places, you'll find
tapped out veins. But if you venture off the beaten path, you'll
improve your chances of discovering new idea lodes.

To be an explorer you must believe that there is a lot of
good information around you, and all you have to do is find it. If
you go to an airport, you'll find ideas there. If you go to a museum, you'll find ideas there as well. And the same applies to
hardware stores, garbage dumps, boutiques, libraries, parking
garages, wilderness areas, restaurants, botanical gardens, and
classrooms. Indeed, the more divergent your sources, the
more original the idea you create is likely to be.

Many good ideas have been discovered because someone
poked around in an outside industry or discipline, and applied
what he found to his own field. Football coach Knute Rockne
got the idea for his "four horsemen" backfield shift while
watching a burlesque chorus routine. World War I military
designers borrowed from the cubist art of Picasso and Braque
to create more efficient camouflage patterns for tanks and
guns. Mathematician John von Neumann analyzed poker-table
behavior and developed the "game theory" model of economics. The roll-on deodorant was an adaptation of the ball point
pen. Drive-in banks were adapted from drive-in restaurants.
I've known songwriters who got inspiration from listening to
crowd chants at basketball games, venture capitalists who
spotted new opportunities by going to junk yards, educators

who got ideas by going to prisons, advertising people who borrowed ideas from biology, and software programmers who were influenced by songwriters. It's not surprising that Thomas Edison gave his colleagues this advice:

Make it a point to keep on the lookout for novel and interesting ideas that others have used successfully. Your idea has to be original only in its adaptation to the problem you are currently working on.

Exercise: Where do you explore for ideas? What outside people, places, activities, and situations do you use to stimulate your thinking?

I've asked many people this question. Here are some of their ideas.

Magic. Through the study and performance of magic, I've learned the power that certain symbols have when they are associated with one another. I've taken this knowledge and applied it to sales and product demonstrations.

Daydreaming to sound effects records. It really sets my mind free.

Junk Yards. Going to a junk yard is a sobering experience. There you can see the ultimate destination of almost everything we desire.

Flea Markets. Flea markets are one of the last outposts of free enterprise. If you want to know what a free economy is all about, go to a flea market. There you can see the values people place on things.

Acting Class. From acting class I have been able to appreciate the impact that positive encouragement has on a person. I have seen some performances that were so bad that I was embarrassed to watch. But the acting coach gave the person criticism in an encouraging way. As a result, these people were able to grow as actors. I think that there is a lesson here for many areas of life.

Old Science Magazines. I get ideas from reading old popular science magazines from the early twentieth century. There were many good ideas proposed then that couldn't be implemented because the materials weren't available then. However, the materials to implement them are available now.

Want Ads. The want ad section of the newspaper is what people are all about—not the front page. In the want ads you see what people want, and what they want to get rid of. This gives me ideas.

Sports. I think sports provides a good source of ideas. I find an interesting parallel between why some teams always win and why some managers are able to motivate people.

History. History is filled with ideas. Napoleon marching on Moscow is really just project management. Mao carrying on a guerrilla war is like launching an advertising campaign.

Nature. In the course of their evolution, natural systems have solved a variety of problems—often in quite ingenious ways. If you look at nature with an eye toward analogy, you'll pick up some good ideas. The sticky hook spine of the common burr inspired the man who invented Velcro fastener. The spinning wheel feature of the elm seed served as a model for more efficient windmills and helicopters. Bell invented the telephone by imitating the ear.

Summary

Specialization is a fact of life. In order to function in the world, you have to narrow your focus and limit your field of view. When you're trying to generate new ideas, however, such information-handling attitudes can limit you. They not only may force you into delimiting your problem too narrowly, they may also prevent you from looking in outside areas for ideas.

TIP: Develop the explorer's attitude: the outlook that wherever you go, there are ideas waiting to be discovered.

TIP: Don't get so busy that you lose the free time necessary for exploring. Give yourself a non-task day once a month or so, or an afternoon every several weeks. When was the last time you went to a junk yard? A sporting event? A television studio? Schedule exploring time into your day and week.

TIP: Read outside your area. Whether it's *Casket & Sunnyside* (magazine of the funeral industry) or *Muscle* magazine, you never know what you'll find in other places.

TIP: Read fiction. It's a great way to stimulate your imagination. One person told me that he likes to read four or five books from different subject areas at the same time in the hope that a book in one area will stimulate his thinking in another. Not long ago, he was reading a management development book on how to motivate people at the same time he was reading *The Godfather* by Mario Puzo. When he finished both of them, he said that he got more motivational insights from the novel than he did from the "how to" book.

TIP: When you "capture" an idea, be sure to write it down.

7. Avoid Ambiguity

Thinking Ambiguously

Exercise: In the following line of letters, cross out six letters so that the remaining letters, without altering their sequence, will spell a familiar English word.

BSAINXLEATNTEARS

Play with it for a while before proceeding.

In the mid-1960's, FBI director J. Edgar Hoover was reading a typed copy of a letter he had just dictated to his secretary. He didn't like the way she had formatted the letter, so he wrote on the bottom, "Watch the borders," and asked her to re-type it. The secretary did as she was instructed and sent it off to all top agents. For the next two weeks FBI agents were put out on special alert along the Canadian and Mexican borders.

This story illustrates two of the main reasons why most people don't like ambiguous situations (those that can be interpreted in more than one way): 1) they're confusing, and 2) they cause communication problems. As a result, we have learned to "avoid ambiguity." This is a good rule to follow for most practical situations such as giving directions, documenting programs, or drawing up contracts. On these occasions it's important to be clear, precise, and specific in order to get your message across.

There are instances, however, when ambiguity can be a powerful stimulant to your imagination. When you're in the imaginative phase of the creative process, a little ambiguity can whack you into asking such questions as:

What's going on here?
What does this mean?
How else can this be interpreted?

These are special questions, the kind you ask when you are looking for new ideas. So, one way to "think something different" is to look at things ambiguously. For example, what is half of 8? One answer is 4. But if you assume that the question is ambiguous, you'll look for other answers such as 0, 3, E, M, and "eig," all depending on how you define "half."

Okay, how did you do with the six letters exercise? What word did you find? Many people look at the problem and say, "Okay, here's a string of sixteen letters, and to solve this problem I should cross out 6 of them. That means I'm looking for a 10 letter word." And that's what they spend their time looking for.

I gave this problem to a person who was an avid computer user. He went home that night and said, "I'll show that Roger. I'll write a program to cross out 6 letters, and have the computer figure out the answer. I'll just take a shower while it does this, and when I get back the answer will be printed out." When he came back, he had a roll of printout thirty feet long containing such glittering possibilities as:

SAINXEAEAR	BSAIXEEARS	BSINLEANEA
BINXLTEARS	AINXLEANAS	BANEATNTER
SINXEATNTE	BAINLATNAR	SNLETNTARS
SANLATNTAR	INXLEANEAR	INXEATEARS
BSNXLENTAT	INLETNTARS	SAIZNTEARS
SABXATNTEA	SINXLETERS	SAILTNTEAR
NLEATNTEAS	IXLEATNTAS	SAINLATEAR
IXLEATTEAR	BIXLETTEAR	BAINEATARS
SNXLETTARS	BSNLENEARS	INEATNTEAR
BSAXLETARS	BLEATTEARS	INXATNTEAR
BAINNEANTS	SXLEATNTES	BINLATTEAR
SNXLEATNRS	ANXLEATNAS	AINLTNTEAR
BAINXATEAR	BAXLEATEAR	BSIXLANERS

As soon as he saw the list, he realized that he had been asking the wrong question. He discovered that you could have the greatest computer on earth, but if you've got the wrong program in it, you'll end up with garbage.

One way to solve this problem is to interpret the instructions with an ambiguous attitude. What else could "cross out six letters" mean? Perhaps instead of crossing out 6 letters, you literally crossed out the "S," and the "I," and the "X," and the "L," and the "E," and so on. If you try this approach, you will be left with the word:

BANANA

My point is this: one way to be more creative is to look for ambiguity in the world around you. The kindergartners who saw the chalk dot as an owl's eye, a cigar butt, a squashed bug had the ability to do this. So did Picasso when he saw the bicycle handle-bars as bull's horns. So did Grace Hopper when she saw eleven inches of string as one nanosecond. And so have you if you've ever used a brick as a doorstop, made chimes out of forks and spoons, used leaves as toilet paper, or used a ball point pen as a hole punch. The ability to find ambiguity is an important part of "thinking something different."

The American General George S. Patton had similar ideas on how to stimulate people's creativity. He said, "If you tell people where to go, but not how to get there, you'll be amazed at the results." He knew that posing a problem in an ambiguous way would give more freedom to the imaginations of the people who were working on the problem.

The renowned Canadian architect Arthur Erickson uses this strategy to unlock his students' creativity. Here's an example of one of his exercises. Give it a try.

Note: Since this book is advocating looking for the second right answer, I should point out that there is at least one other solution to this problem. If you choose six different letters–say "B," "S," "A," "I," "N," and "X"–and cross them out every time they appear, you would end up with the word "LETTER."

Exercise: Draw a picture of yourself in a position of movement, and then provide a device (made out of plastic, wood, paper, or metal) to support that position.

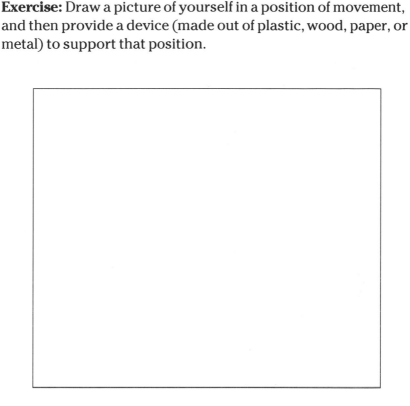

At the end of the exercise, Erickson points out to his students that they have been designing furniture. As he puts it: "If I had said to the students, 'Look, we're going to design a chair or a bed,' they would have explored the design on the basis of previous memories of chairs and beds. But by approaching the model from the opposite and essential direction, I was able to make them realize the vital aspects of furniture."

As you can see, sometimes all you need is a dose or two of amibiguity to whack your thinking into high gear. Thus, I'd like to prescribe a few of the following sources of ambiguity to you.

Paradoxes

This chapter is paradoxical. On the one hand, I've said that ambiguity causes communications problems. On the other, I've said that it helps create new ideas. What's the common denominator? Both situations stimulate you to think.

That's probably the reason why, in the midst of a difficult problem, the Danish physicist Niels Bohr was overheard to say, "How wonderful that we've met with a paradox. Now we have hope of making some progress." Bohr knew that paradoxes are crucial to the creative process. That's because they whack you out of narrow thought paths and force you to question your assumptions. Indeed, the very act of "seeing the paradox" is at the crux of creative thinking—the ability to entertain two different, often contradictory, notions at the same time.

I'd like to share some of my favorites with you:

◆ The little I know I owe to my ignorance.

◆ There is nothing so unthinkable as thought unless it be the entire absence of thought.
—*Samuel Butler*

◆ Barbara Gorman was disappointed to find no suggestion box in the clubhouse because she would like to put a suggestion in it about having one.
—*Diane Campbell*

◆ Any company large enough to have a research lab is too large to listen to it.
—*Alan Kay*

◆ Only the ephemeral is of lasting value.
—*Ionesco*

◆ The notes I handle no better than many pianists. But the pauses between notes—ah, that is where the art resides.
—*Arthur Schnabel*

◆ A physicist is an atom's way of knowing about atoms.
—*George Wald*

◆ There are two kinds of truth, small truth and great truth. You can recognize a small turth because its opposite is a falsehood. The opposite of a great truth is another great truth.
—*Niels Bohr*

◆ Whenever I'm accosted by panhandlers, I give them a little printed card that says, "I'm sorry, but I spent all of my spare change having these cards printed."
—*Bob Wieder*

◆ If you can remember the 60's, then you weren't there.
—*Timothy Leary*

◆ We can't leave the haphazard to chance.
—*N.F. Simpson*

◆ Art is a lie that makes us realize the truth.
—*Pablo Picasso*

Consult An Oracle

Many cultures have developed tools that take advantage of our ability to make sense out of ambiguous situations. These tools are called oracles. Some examples include: the ancient Chinese *I Ching,* the Egyptian Tarot, the Nordic Runes, and the North American Indian Medicine Wheel. Traditionally, the purpose of using these oracles was not so much to foretell the future, as it was to enable the user to delve deeper into his own intuition when dealing with a problem.

Probably the most famous source of ambiguous pronouncements was the oracle at Delphi in the ancient world. One of the oracle's best known prophecies came in the year 480 B.C. The Persians under Xerxes had invaded the Greek mainland and had successfully conquered two-thirds of the country. Naturally, the Athenian city-fathers were concerned as to which course of action they should take against the on-coming Persians. They realized, however, that before any decision could be made, they should send some suppliants to Delphi to get a reading from the oracle. The suppliants made the journey and received the following prophecy:

The wooden wall will save you and your children.

The suppliants took these words back to Athens. At first, the city-fathers were unsure what the prophecy meant. Then one person suggested that they should build a wooden wall up on the Acropolis and take a defensive stand behind it. That's what the "wooden wall" meant—a barricade on the Acropolis.

But the city-fathers knew that the oracle was intentionally ambiguous to force them to go beyond the first right answer. They tried to think of all of the contexts—both literal and metaphorical—in which the words "the wooden wall will save you and your children" would make some sense. After some thought, they came up with another idea. Could the "wooden wall" to which the oracle was referring be the result of all of the

Athenian wooden-hulled ships lined up next to one another?
From a distance, the ships would indeed look like a wooden
wall. The city-fathers decided, therefore, that the battle should
be a naval one rather than a land one.

   In 479 B.C., the Athenians went on to rout the Persians in
the Battle of Salamis. The oracle's ambiguity forced the Athenians to consult the deeper wisdom of their own intuition, and
consider alternatives.

What do you do if you want to tap into your intuition but can't get to Delphi? Why not create your own oracle. It's really quite simple. The following story gives the basic principles at work.

There once was an Indian medicine man whose responsibilities included creating hunting maps for his tribe. Whenever game got sparse, he'd lay a piece of fresh leather out in the sun to dry. Then he'd fold and twist it in his hands, say a few prayers over it, and smooth it out. The rawhide was now criss-crossed with lines and wrinkles. The medicine man marked some basic reference points on the rawhide, and—presto!— a new game map was created. The wrinkles represented new trails the hunters should follow. When the hunters followed the map's newly defined trails, they invariably discovered abundant game.

Moral: By allowing the rawhide's random folds to represent hunting trails, he pointed the hunters to places they previously had not looked.

You can create an oracle in the same way the medicine man did. You'll need to do three things:

1. Ask a question. (The medicine man asked: "Where can more game be found?") This question focuses your thinking.

2. Generate a random piece of information. (The medicine man twisted and folded a piece of leather.) The random selection is important. Since people tend to use the same problem-solving approaches repeatedly, they

come up with the same answers. Since a random piece
of information is unpredictable, it forces you to look at
the problem in a new way.

3. Interpret the resulting random piece of information
as the answer to your question. (The medicine man
interpreted lines as representing new hunting trails.)

If you have a question and an open, receptive mind, then you're two-thirds of the way toward creating an oracle. Let's run through it step by step.

1. Let's suppose that you're working on a project and wonder, "What should I be thinking about? What should I do next? What's an alternative approach? What aren't I seeing?" First off, clear your mind. Take time to relax and focus your thinking. Now form your question.

2. Select something from the world at random. Indeed, constructing the means to get a piece of unexpected information can be both a great way to use your imagination and a lot of fun. It could be one of the following:

*Pick out the sixth word on page 247 of your dictionary: *A doorknob.*

*Open a magazine. Count the the 12th full page advertisement from the front. What product is shown? *An exercise machine.*

*Look out the window and find the second thing that has yellow in it: *A tennis ball.*

*Open a catalog at random. What's in the upper left hand corner? *Coffee cups.*

*Go to the center of your town or city and walk north exactly 1.6 miles. Enter a store on the right hand side. Find the strongest smelling item you can find: *Second hand dresses that have been stored away in moth balls.*

*Open up the stock section of your newspaper. Go to the third column. Count down to the 16th company whose shares increased in value the previous day. What is their main product? *Water faucets.*

*It could be a word that you pick at random on the next page.

maze anvil bait balloon nail key organ skin zone pump parachute program quilt rag powder harbor vertebra glue hair raft lode ruler kitchen robot valley plate mountain needle violin pacemaker soap pen knife piano planet pocket dung powder pump radar halo rubber saddle cup school ship road ball zoo trigger cloud chord chain cannon caldron man woman crystal channel copy cycle plow egg hook drain drum tree bomb wing furniture fungus fork fog flood guitar flag treasure water well girdle glue hair template mirror camera wedge wave sandpaper chessboard desert crown clock cinema food cave staircase network bridge water dust eraser statue net gate pump broom bottleneck ratchet-wheel glacier funhouse fossil block food flower floor antenna god guillotine bee plug blanket funnel book brain brakes booby-trap cesspool cell cancer weed buffer toilet television spring tub compass circle code web dress current detour ear button face factory fairy fan farm feather fertilizer field finger engine floodlight sandwich treasure cup umbrella farm feather fertilizer spectrum template forge adult dope color hole bottle bird trap foot fly foam game garden gear ghost glass graph gun gutter bruise bug circus hammer head heart family blister acid candy chorus springboard fire film festival fence fish eye drill body die spotlight frame glove hand song grave lever sphere square sun table tool trail vent vegetable soup spiral shaft market torpedo thermometer ticket vacuum triangle train torch sword weirdness telescope target spear sponge stomach memory spectrum telephone tapestry kaleidoscope car stove skeleton room treadmill oven filter root temple window star typewriter seed bed fountain armor battery molecule purse library fruit water air earth money spice bell rock album robot farm weapon bank tide bag computer army diamond altar tunnel amoeba anvil bait bible hinge image junk knot sex match manual liquid leg lamp algebra alphabet menu prison monster nest nut opium page parasite pendulum microscope radio puzzle prism port ring pod satellite pill pepper rainbow rudder safe sauce saloon shadow shovel smoke rash horizon mattress map machine lock lever landslide ladder index key ice meteor mist moon music net ocean sphere paint passport perfume river rope pipe plant pond pore prison pyramid record rope rug sand saw screw shell signature herb hose icon horoscope star meat march magnet lode vise nail meter missle motor organ nose onion palette pebble script shoe siren house lightning bridge network eraser laser lens milk mask medal thunder bomb fungus fog soap kite music prison blister toilet pill lode ramp saddle vulture water dust gear blanket garden song rug hook pen knife fork rash weed scale loom rubber hinge ladle landslide lever lock machine mattress copy umbrella hair template farm crystal fossil wedge wave torch root window battery lever keys sponge stomach memory spectrum telephone tapestry kaleidoscope car stove skeleton room treadmill oven filter root temple window star typewriter seed bed fountain armor gutter bruise bug circus hammer head heart family blister acid candy chorus parachute template mountain needle violin pacemaker soap pen knife piano planet pocket dung powder pump radar halo rubber saddle cup school ship road ball rudder safe sauce saloon shadow shovel smoke lamp leg ocean muscle cycle meteor funnel fork rain loans fly dust oven temple star typewriter weapon machine pendulum path objective pool onion treasure fog camera fungus candy shovel torpedo knife planet life stone shell chapter classroom dump robot farm weapon bank tide bag computer army diamond altar tunnel amoeba valley plate sandwich treasure cup stove skeleton room treadmill oven filter root temple window star typewriter seed bed foam game garden gear ghost glass graph gun gutter bruise bug circus hammer head sea herb gangster partner fascist halo nerd trend computer guerilla copy tomb womb comb broom thumb finger footprint palm lotus blossom fool window carpet luck dictionary parasite trashcan door button smudge pimple horseshoe pen thorn suitcase desktop appliance car oracle crown clock cinema food cave staircase network parachute template mountain needle violin pacemaker soap pen knife piano planet pocket dung powder pump radar voicebox finger molecule pod script meat puzzle tunnel amoeba eyeball ear wedge dung meteor oven loins testicles ovaries umbrella magic duality partner game wave fork wristwatch keys blister crystal gridlock logjam corn tomato paper pirate roof fence telephone rock'n'roll compass circle code web dress current detour ear button face factory fairy fan farm engine floodlight sandwich treasure cup umbrella farm feather fertilizer spectrum template forge adult dope color hole bottle bird trap foot fly foam game garden gear ghost glass graph gun gutter bruise bug circus hammer head heart family book cup album robot farm weapon camera wedge wave sandpaper chessboard desert crown clock cave staircase network map machine lock lever landslide ladder index moon music net ocean sphere earthquake watch ear lever lock machine mattress oracle

3. Now think how the random thing applies to your situation. Take as much time as you need. There is a connection between the random thing you select and your problem—and your job is to find it. As stated above, we humans are quite good at finding patterns and meaning in the world around us—even if none was intended. Thus, whatever you find will have a way of adding insight into your problem and providing clarification.

What are different ways in which it relates to or could apply to your question?

Be creative.

Go beyond your first answer; look for a second and a third and a fifth right answer.

Be literal in your interpretation.

Be metaphorical.

Be off-the-wall.

Be serious.

Think of each random thing as a stimulant to your imagination. Let it spark a series of fresh associations in your mind. Like pebbles dropping in a pond, they will stimulate other associations, some of which may help you find or think of something new.

Don't worry how practical or logical you are. What's important is where each random thing leads you.

Most will trigger an immediate response. Sometimes, however, you'll look at one and think, "This doesn't have anything to do with my problem," and be tempted to reject it and reach for a new one. Don't do it. Force yourself to make a connection. Believe that one way or another everything—whether it's cow's milk or anti-war riots, church services or dried flowers, soap bubbles or knight's armor—is connected to everything else.

Remember: often those ideas that initially seem the least relevant become the most important ones of all because they point to something that you've been completely overlooking.

For example, if "mothballs" or "water faucets" aren't the typical things you think of when dealing with a problem, then your responses to these ideas are likely to give you new insight into your question.

into your question.

When should you consult your oracle for another random idea? When you've finished the current one. It might be right now, or it might be next week.

A True-Life Example. Owen Dennis is a resident of Christchurch, New Zealand. Several years ago, it was his job to promote the annual parish fair for his church. He wanted to do something different, something that would really get people's attention. He thought and thought, but nothing amazing came to him. Finally, he decided to pose the problem to an oracle. The problem: "How can I promote my church fund-raiser." The oracle he chose was this book (the very one you're holding in your hands). He said I'll flip this book open at random. The picture on that page will be the answer to my question. The picture he got was on page 34 of the two workmen climbing up the ladders for the Soft and Hard Association Quiz. Owen thought to himself, "That's my answer!" Now he had to figure out what it meant. He finally got a picture in his mind of the Vicar of his church climbing a ladder up to the bell tower of St. Anne's (13 meters above the ground). He then got the idea that the Vicar, Reverend Simon Ballantyne, would spend forty-eight hours in the bell tower— "a step nearer heaven." Owen talked the Vicar into the stunt. He further promoted it by comparing it to a feat performed by the fourth century ascetic Simeon Stylites, who preached from the top of a pole for thirty-one years. Accompanied by several "good books" and a ham radio, the Vicar survived the stunt in good spirits. His promotion helped the fair raise over $6,000.

Let a random piece of information stimulate your thinking.

Listen to Your Dreams

To those who are awake, there is one ordered universe, whereas in sleep each person turns away from this world to one of his own.

—Heraclitus, Philosopher

Your dreams are another profound source of ambiguity. How many mornings have you awakened and thought, "What in the world was that dream all about? Why did I dream of catching bugs with a toothbrush? What did it mean that I shot my boss or someone kidnapped my child?" But if you take time to write the dream down and interpret it, you may discover something interesting that will lead your thinking in a whole new direction.

Exercise: Remember a dream you've had recently (or tonight, tell yourself to remember your dream and write it down immediately upon awakening). Now ask yourself these questions:

◆ How do you feel in the dream? (Afraid, strong, vulnerable, in love, crazy, alienated, confident.)

◆ How do you feel about the dream? (Relieved, embarrassed, excited, confused, surprised.)

◆ Who is in the dream? (An old lover, Kermit the Frog, a teacher, a movie star, the Emperor of Japan, a burglar.)

◆ Where does it take place? (At home, in Russia, in your elementary school, on the planet Jupiter.)

◆ How do the different people react to what happens in the dream? (Do they run, act silly, take their clothes off, or discover a cure for cancer?)

◆ What is unusual? (People float, you can speak Italian, animals communicate telepathically.)

Now interpret these self-generated picture stories. Think of them as symbols through which your unconscious mind is speaking to you. Think of them as you would an oracle. Go beyond your first right answer and look for a second and a third. If you dream someone kidnaps your children, you might take it as a sign that you should spend more time with them. It might also mean that you believe someone is stealing your ideas. Or perhaps it could mean that you're being too serious (your childlike side has been abducted) and therefore you should be more playful.

If you dream of death, it doesn't necessarily mean the person has died, but that what they represent to you is gone. Pregnancy could signify a new project or idea you're conceiving.

You may dream of school and all that entails: losing your homework, being late for class, or missing a test. This may reflect a new situation in which you feel like a student again, and parts of your performance are inadequate or out of control.

Your dream may lead you to a new furniture design, a different way of dealing with your manager, or you may get an insight into a problem much in the same way nineteenth century inventor Elias Howe did. His dream of being attacked by spears with holes through their points led him to change the design of the needle in his sewing machine (he put the eye near the point instead of its traditional position at the other end).

You may also get a fresh insight into yourself or how you look at other people. My daughter dreamed that giants were chasing her. The only escape was through a small square hole in a door. Her grandmother said, "No, we can't make it," but Athena said, "Yes, we can if we wiggle like this," and they escaped. She woke up feeling good about herself knowing that her ingenuity and persistence had helped her solve a problem. My wife has had a series of dreams of being in a theater. During the course of ten years she has moved from being in the audience, to part of the chorus, to serving as an understudy, to being the star, to writing her own script.

Remember: your dreams are uniquely yours. Take advantage of them to help you resolve conflicts, inspire solutions, and suggest new approaches. How can you relate a recent dream to a current problem?

Heraclitus

Finally, I believe that everyone should have his own personal source of ambiguity. This could be a person, a book, a thing—whatever—that forces you to look for more than one meaning in order to understand what's going on. One of mine is the ancient Greek philosopher Heraclitus who lived about the fifth century B.C. Even to his contemporaries, he was known as the "Obscure One." Here are some of his thoughts:

- Everything flows.

- It is not possible to step into the same river twice.

- Sea water is the purest and most polluted: for fish it is drinkable and life-giving. For men, not drinkable and destructive.

- They do not understand how that which differs with itself is in agreement: harmony consists of opposing tension, like that of the lyre and the bow.

- The way up and the way down are one and the same.

- If all things turned to smoke, the nose would be the discriminating organ.

- If you don't expect the unexpected you will not reach it, for it is not to be reached by search or trail.

- There await men after they are dead things that they do not expect or imagine.

- Time is a child playing draughts: the kingship is in the hands of the child.

- It is not good for men to achieve all they wish.

- Man is most nearly himself when he achieves the seriousness of a child at play.

- A man's character is his destiny.

- I searched into myself.

- Lovers of wisdom must be inquirers into very many things indeed.

I've been reading Heraclitus for over twenty years, and he never fails to stimulate my thinking. I suggest that you seek out your own source of ambiguity and cultivate it as a valuable resource.

Summary

Most of us have learned to "avoid ambiguity" because of the communication problems it can cause. This is an especially good idea in practical situations where the consequences of such a misunderstanding would be serious. For example, a fire chief fighting a three-alarm fire needs to issue his orders with utmost clarity so as to leave nothing to question.

In imaginative situations, however, there is the danger that too much specificity can stifle your imagination. Let's suppose that the same fire chief has asked you to paint a mural on the side of his firehouse. If he tells you what he wants it to look like right down to the last detail, he hasn't given you any room for your imagination. Perhaps, if the assignment were stated somewhat ambiguously, then you would have more room to think and be creative. In other words, there is a place for ambiguity—perhaps not so much when you're evaluating and executing ideas, but certainly when you're searching for and playing with them.

TIP: Take advantage of the ambiguity in the world. Look at something and think about what else it might be.

TIP: If you're giving someone a problem that has the potential of being solved in a creative way, then you might try—at least initially—posing it in an ambiguous fashion so as not to restrict their imagination.

TIP: Cultivate your own sources of ambiguity. These could be people, books, things—whatever—that force you to look for more than one meaning in order to understand what's going on.

TIP: Let the world be your oracle. Allow random, unexpected information to stimulate your imagination.

TIP: Listen to your dreams.

8. Don't Be Foolish

Going Along

The nail that sticks up will be hammered down.

—Japanese Proverb

Scene #1. A man walks into the waiting room of a doctor's office. He looks around and is surprised by what he sees: everybody is in their underwear. People are drinking coffee in their underwear, reading magazines in their underwear, and carrying on conversations in their underwear. He's shocked at first, but then decides that they must know something he doesn't. After about twenty seconds, he also takes off his clothes and sits down in his underwear.

Scene #2. A woman waits patiently for an elevator in an office building. After a short period, the elevator arrives and the doors open. As she looks in, she notices that everybody is turned around and facing to the rear of the elevator. So, she, too, gets into the elevator and faces the rear.

These scenes are from Allen Funt's 1960's television series *Candid Camera.* They both confirm what countless psychology tests have found, namely, the best way to get along is to go along.

All of us are subject to group pressures. Study your own behavior, and you'll see how much you conform to various situations. Let's suppose that you're driving down the freeway, and everyone around you is going ten miles per hour over the speed limit. What happens? It's very difficult not to break the law—you get caught up in the "flow of traffic." Suppose that you are a pedestrian standing at the corner of an intersection in a major city. Ten or twelve other people are standing there with you. The sign says, "DON'T WALK," but no traffic is coming. Then one of the pedestrians crosses the street against the light. Soon another goes, and then another. In no time, all the other pedestrians have crossed the street against the light.

And you do too, because you would feel really stupid being the only person still standing there.

Let's suppose you're standing in a checkout line in a grocery store. The other people in line are standing silently facing the cash register. What do you do? Do you tell them about your theory of the tri-partite nature of the soul? Do you ask them what their favorite colors are? Do you start making chicken noises? No, you look straight ahead and keep your mouth shut because that's what people do in checkout lines. After all, you don't want to look foolish, do you?

Benefits of Conformity

Conformity serves several practical purposes. First, living in society requires your cooperation with other people. Without conformity, traffic would get tied up, production quotas would be missed, and the fabric of society would come apart. Part of the price you pay for the benefits of your social existence is a piece of your own individuality. There are hundreds, if not thousands, of rituals you go through in which your behavior must conform to the people around you—everything from how you pronounce words so that you effectively communicate to driving on the proper side of the road to assure smooth traffic flow. If you don't conform, not only might you throw a monkey-wrench in the gears of society, you also run the risk of appearing stupid—like you don't know what's going on.

Second, in those situations where you don't know your way around, what do you do? You look to others for the right way to act. Suppose you're in a laundromat, and you're not quite sure how to operate the washing machine. What do you do? Probably look over to the person next to you and try the approach that person is using. Similarly, I once watched my then four year old son watch a *Three Stooges* movie. For the most part, he sat silently trying to figure out what was going on. The next day when he watched the movie with his seven year old sister, he laughed at all the same places that she did. In this way, he was developing a sophisticated sense of humor.

My favorite example of conformity is a story about St. Augustine. As a young priest in Milan, he went to his bishop, Ambrose, for help with a problem. It seemed that Augustine was going to spend the weekend in Rome. His problem was that in Rome it was customary to celebrate the Sabbath on Sunday, while in Milan it was celebrated on Saturday. Augustine was confused as to which was the appropriate day. Ambrose solved Augustine's problem by telling him:

When in Rome, do as the Romans do.

Groupthink

New ideas, however, are not born in a conforming environment. Whenever people get together, there is the danger of "groupthink." This is the phenomenon in which group members are more interested in getting the approval of the others rather than trying to come up with creative solutions to the problems at hand. Thus, when everyone thinks alike, no one is doing very much thinking.

Alfred Sloan knew the dangers of groupthink. In the late 1930's, Sloan was chairing a board meeting at General Motors. An idea was proposed and everybody became very enthusiastic about it. One person said, "We'll make a lot of money with this proposal." Another said, "Let's implement it as soon as possible." And still another said, "We'll knock the pants off our competition." After the discussion, Sloan said, "It's now time to vote on the proposal." The vote went around the table, and one by one, each board member voted "Aye." When the vote came back to Sloan, he said, "I, too, vote 'Aye' and that makes it unanimous. And for that reason, I'm going to table the motion until next month. I don't like what's happening to our thinking. We're getting locked into looking at this idea in just one way, and this is a dangerous way to make decisions. I want each of you to spend the next month studying this proposal from a different perspective." A month went by, and the proposal was brought up again. This time, however, it was voted down. The board members had had an opportunity to break through the effects of groupthink.

Similarly, I remember in the mid-1970's visiting my cousin, a farmer, in North Dakota. He showed me a freshly constructed pig cellar for breeding pigs. It was beautiful. I asked him if he was happy about it. He replied, "I would be except that the building inspector told me that everywhere he goes he sees people putting in pig cellars. That means that in eighteen months there will be a glut and prices will go down." Sure enough, a year and a half later, prices for his pork products plummeted.

Consult A Fool

Any decision-maker (and we all are) has to deal with the problem of conformity and groupthink. But how? Why not do what decision-makers and problem-solvers since the dawn of civilization have done to stimulate their imaginations and improve their judgment:

Ask a fool what he thinks.

Looking at the fool's wildly colored clothing and donkey-eared cap, it's easy to regard him as a simpleton, an imbecile whose proverbial "elevator doesn't go all the way to the top floor," or a moron "whose bell has no clapper." Don't be fooled! The classical fool is no dunce. It takes intelligence, imagination, cleverness, and insight to play this role. A good fool needs to be part actor and part poet, part philosopher and part psychologist.

The fool was consulted by Egyptian pharaohs and Babylonian kings. His opinion was sought by Roman emperors and Greek tyrants. He advised Indian chiefs in the Pueblo, Zuni, and Hopi nations. He played an important role at the courts of the Chinese emperors. The fool was prominently employed by European royalty in the Middle Ages and Renaissance. Because of his ability to open up people's thinking, the fool has been held in as much esteem as the priest, the medicine man, and the shaman.

What did the fool do? Simply stated, it was his job to whack the king's (pharaoh, emperor, chief, decision-maker, problem-solver, etc.) thinking out of habitual thought patterns. The king's advisers were often "yes-men"—they told him exactly what he wanted to hear. The king realized that this wasn't a good way to make decisions. Therefore, he gave the fool a *license* to parody any proposal under discussion and to shatter the prevailing mindset. The fool's candid jokes and off-beat observations put the issue in a fresh light and forced the king to re-examine his assumptions. By listening to the fool, the king improved his judgment, enhanced his creativity, and protected himself from groupthink.

The fool operates in a world that runs counter to conventional patterns. Everyday ways of perceiving, understanding, and acting have little meaning for him. He'll extol the trivial, trifle the exalted, and parody the common perception of a situation. Here are some examples of the fool's approach:

The fool will reverse our standard assumptions. He might say, "If a man is sitting on a horse facing the rear, why do we assume that it is the man who is backwards and not the horse?"

He is irreverant. He'll pose a riddle such as, "What is it that the rich man puts in his pocket that the poor man throws away?" When he answers, "Snot," he forces you to re-examine the sanctity of your most basic daily rituals.

He might deny that a problem even exists and therefore reframe the situation. Most people think recessions are bad. Not the fool. The fool says, "Recessions are good. They make people work more efficiently. People work harder when they are insecure about the future of their jobs. Also, most companies have a fair amount of fat in them. Recessions force them to trim back to their fighting weight and be more agressive."

The fool can be absurd. Having lost his donkey, a fool got down on his knees and began thanking God. A passerby saw him and asked, "Your donkey is missing; what are thanking God for?" The fool replied, "I'm thanking Him for seeing to it that I wasn't riding him at the time. Otherwise, I would be missing too."

The fool notices things that other people overlook. He might ask, "Why do people who pour cream into their coffee do so after the coffee is already in the cup,

rather than pouring the cream in first and saving themselves the trouble of stirring?"

The fool is metaphorical. When answering the following question on an intelligence test: "Which is
true: A) Birds eat seeds, or B) Seeds eat birds," he might
answer both A and B because he has seen dead birds on
the ground decompose into the soil to fertilize freshly
planted seeds.

The fool will apply the rules of one arena to another.
He'll go to a football game and imagine he's in
church. He'll see the players huddling and think they're
praying. He'll see the vendors in the stands and think
that they're taking up a collection. He'll see the fans'
hero worship of the star quarterback and imagine that
he's witnessing the Second Coming.

The fool can be cryptic. He'll say the best way to see
something is with your ears. Initially, this may seem
a little weird, but after you've thought about it, you just
might agree that *listening* to a poem or short story
conjures up more images in your mind than *watching*
television.

The great physicist Niels Bohr felt that thinking like a fool
was essential to coming up with breakthrough ideas. While in
the midst of a tense brainstorming session, he told a colleague:

We all know your idea is crazy. The question is, whether it is crazy enough.

The great benefit of the fool's antics and observations is
that they stimulate your thinking. They jolt your mind in the
same way that a splash of cold water wakes you up when
you're drowsy. You may not like the fool's ideas. Some of them

may even irritate you or strike you as silly or useless. But he forces you to entertain—perhaps only momentarily—an alternative way of looking at your situation. Whatever assumptions you hold must be suspended. The fool's approach to life jars you into an awareness that there is a second right answer to what you're doing, and that you should look for better answers than the ones you've got.

This approach is important. In a time when things are changing very quickly, who is to say what's right and what's foolish. As Albert Einstein once said:

A question that sometimes drives me hazy: Am I or are the others crazy?

Indeed, sometimes the fool makes more sense than the wise man. Some of the most foolish ideas from five years ago are now a reality.

Put On Your Fool's Cap

If anyone among you thinks he is
wise in this age, let him become
a fool that he may become wise.

–I Corinthians iii, 18-19

What if you don't have a fool around to help you? Why not give yourself a license to be foolish. You're smart, right? You've got a sense of humor, right? Go ahead and put on your fool's cap. You'll find that it cleanses your judgment and opens up your mind. Don't worry about people who say "don't be foolish." After all, you know that thinking like a fool is for a good purpose. Dig into your fool's bag of tricks. Look at the problem before you and say, "It's not what everyone thinks it is," and give a different interpretation of what's going on. Deny that the problem even exists, or maybe solve a different one. Doubt the things that others take for granted. Ridicule your basic assumptions. Expected the unexpected. Ask the stupid question that nobody else seems to be asking. Do whatever you can to shatter the prevailing mindset. You'll find that it will stimulate your creative juices.

Remember those situations when you put on your fool's cap? What happened? Did you come up with a lot of different ideas? Were you more creative? Did you take more risks? Did you have more fun? I'm sure that the answer to all of these questions is "yes." From my own experience I've found that the most effective creative thinking sessions I've conducted were those in which the participants allowed themselves to be foolish.

Here are several of the fool's favorite tools.

Reverse Your Viewpoint

In the late 1950's, a mysterious phenomenon occurred in Seattle: people began discovering small pockmarks on their car windshields. As more and more of these tiny indented scars were found, a kind of mass hysteria developed. Two main theories arose to explain the cause of the pitting. One was that atomic tests by the Russians had contaminated the atmosphere, and this, combined with Seattle's moist climate, had produced fallout that was returning to earth in a glass-etching dew. The other theory was that Seattle's recently constructed roads, again with the help of the foggy dew, were flinging acid drops against the windshields. As the situation became more serious, the Federal government sent a team of experts to investigate the mystery. What they discovered was that there was *no increase* in windshield pitting in Seattle at all. As the reports of the windshield pits came to the attention of more and more people, they began to check their own cars. Most did this by looking through the glass from the outside of the car instead of from the inside. This revealed the pitting that is almost invariably caused by normal wear on a windshield. What had broken out in Seattle was an epidemic not of windshield pitting, but of *reverse windshield viewing*. People reversed their view of the windshield and discovered something that had always been there but they'd never noticed.

This story illustrates what can happen when you reverse your point of view. The fool believes that thinking about and doing things opposite from your customary way allows you to discover the things you typically overlook.

For example, when everyone else is gazing at a gorgeous sunset, why not turn around to see the blues and violets behind you? What do you notice when you look at a coffee cup? Its color? Its material? Its design? Reverse your focus and look at the empty space inside the cup. Isn't that what gives it its functional value?

Reversing your perspective is a good technique for opening up your thinking. Here's an example. For many years, 19th century English physician Edward Jenner worked to find a cure for small pox. After studying many cases, he reached an impasse in his thinking. Then he reversed his perception of the problem. Instead of focusing on people who had small pox, he switched his attention to people who never had small pox. He found that dairy maids rarely got the disease. It turned out that most dairy maids had had cow pox, a similar but usually nonfatal affliction. Cow pox had served to "vaccinate" its victims against the more dangerous small pox. This led to Jenner's concept of "vaccinating" people.

You might also try reversing the order in which you do a particular operation in a project. Designer Christopher Williams tells the following story about an architect who built a cluster of large office buildings that were set in a central green. When construction was completed, the landscape crew asked him where he wanted the sidewalks between the buildings. "Not yet," was the architect's reply. "Just plant the grass solidly between the buildings." This was done, and by late summer the new lawn was laced with pathways of trodden grass, connecting building to building, and building to outside. As Williams puts it, "The paths followed the most efficient line between the points of connection, turned in easy curves rather than right angles, and were sized according to traffic flow. In the fall, the architect simply paved in the pathways. Not only did the pathways have a design beauty, but they responded directly to user needs."

Doing the opposite of what's expected can also be an effective strategy in such competitive situations such as sports, business, warfare, romance, etc. In most endeavors, we build up certain expectations about what the other side will or won't do. In football, for example, a third and one situation will typically cause the defense to prepare for a plunge into the line. In retailing, you can bet that stores will do a lot of advertising between Thanksgiving and Christmas. In politics, most candidates will have a last minute media blitz. In these situations, trends get established. When you do the opposite of what people are expecting, chances are good that you'll catch them off-guard and be more successful in reaching your objective.

Psychiatrist Paul Watzlawick tells the following delightful

story in which doing the unexpected worked in a wartime
situation. In 1334, the Duchess of Tyrol laid siege to the castle
of Hochosterwitz in Austria. She knew that the siege would take
some months because the fortress was located on a cliff high
above the valley floor. As time wore on, the defenders in the
castle became desperate; their only remaining food was an ox
and several bags of grain. The Duchess's situation, however,
had also become severe; her troops were becoming unruly,
there seemed to be no end to the siege, and she had pressing
matters elsewhere.

    At this point, the castle's commander hit upon a plan of
action that must have seemed utter lunacy to his men. He had
the last ox slaughtered, stuffed with grain, and then had the
carcass thrown over the cliff onto the meadow in front of the
enemy camp. The Duchess interpreted this scornful message
to mean that the castle had so much food they could afford to
throw some down. Because the castle's commander did the
opposite of what the Duchess expected, he jolted her into be-
lieving that her siege wasn't working. Thereupon, the discour-
aged Duchess abandoned her siege and moved on.

As innovator Andrew Mercer once put it,

You can't see the good ideas behind you by looking twice as hard at what's in front of you.

Try switching your objective and going in the opposite direction. Suppose you're a teacher and you wonder, "How can I be less effective?" This would mean that the student would have to take more responsibility for her learning, and this could lead to the development of a self-study go-at-your-own-pace program.

Suppose you're a basketball coach and you ask, "How can I get my team out-of-sync?" Your answer might be a list of things that would unsettle them. Then you could practice these things, because they might have to deal with them in a game.

Suppose you're in a grocery store buying produce. You see people around you jamming lettuce, cauliflower, grapes, and broccoli into various plastic bags. You ask yourself, "What if I did this backwards? What if I put my *hand* in the bag, and then grabbed the produce and pulled the bag over it?"

Reversing your viewpoint is a great way to sharpen your thinking. Try disagreeing with people whose ideas, principles, and beliefs you usually agree. You may find that the opposite view makes more sense. If you don't have anyone handy to disagree with you, why not disagree with yourself? Play the fool and take the contrary position on common sense proverbs.

"If something's worth doing, it's worth doing well." If a thing's worth doing, it's okay to do it poorly. Otherwise, you'll never give yourself permission to be a beginner at a new activity. If you have to do well, then you'll prevent yourself from trying new things.

"A chain is no stronger than its weakest link."
Weak links are wonderful! As a matter of fact, many systems have weak links designed into them. They're called "fuses." When a system gets overloaded, the fuse blows and saves the rest of the system. After all, which part do you want to break: the $50,000 piece or the 5¢ one?

"A bird in the hand is worth two in the bush."
Two in the bush are great. After all, everybody needs a dream. Without the "two in the bush" mentality, what would happen to risk-taking?

Exercise: Take one of your favorite pieces of common sense and roast it. You might try some of the following:

1. Business before pleasure.
2. Every cloud has a silver lining.
3. Every dog has its day.
4. Don't put all your eggs in one basket.
5. Fight fire with fire.
6. Patience is a virtue.
7. Haste makes waste.
8. He who laughs last laughs best.
9. Curiosity killed the cat.
10. Beauty is only skin-deep.
11. Tomorrow is another day.
12. If at first you don't succeed, try, try again.
13. As you sow, so you reap.
14. Look before you leap.
15. You can't teach an old dog new tricks.
16. The proof of the pudding is in the eating.
17. Every cloud has a silver lining.
18. Lightning never strikes twice in the same place.
19. As you make your bed, so you must sleep in it.
20. Too many cooks spoiled the broth.

The Fools and the Rules

Finally, the fool loves to parody the rules. In my seminars, I provide an opportunity for participants to do just that. We play a game called the "Fools and the Rules." It's easy to play. You take your holiest sacred cow and sacrifice it on the altar of foolishness. In a perverse sort of way, sometimes the fool makes more sense than the rule. Here are some examples:

RULE: "Always be polite on the telephone."

FOOL: "Are you kidding? Abusive behavior cuts down on phone time. It also gives our public relations department more work. It would eliminate the hold button on the telephone as well as lead to honest employee relationships. Finally, rude telephone manners could serve as an outlet for employee stress."

RULE: "Always communicate through the proper chain of command so as not to surprise your boss."

FOOL: "That's a waste of time. After all, bosses like surprises—they're fun! This would remove any chance for preconceptions (and we all know that preconceptions get in the way of creative ideas). This would also demonstrate how much goes on without anyone knowing. In addition, you would be provided with a means of visibility because you'd continually be called on to the carpet."

RULE: "We will design state-of-the-art products."

FOOL: "Who needs state-of-the-art products? They create state-of-the-art problems. Why not let someone else be the innovator and then we'll copy what they've done. It would be cheaper."

RULE: "Our company is 'Committed to Excellence.'"

FOOL: "How about 'committed to incompetence.' Think of the possibilities! We'd have less development time, lower training costs, and no backlogs. Part shortages wouldn't hold up production. Not only that, we would improve our chances of reaching our design goals. Also—we wouldn't be afraid to try new ideas—after all, what would we have to lose?

"In the past we've been able to sell our products based on their technical merits. With mediocre products, however, we'd have to learn how to sell. We'd also have a larger market: there are more mediocre people in the world than excellent ones. But we would be successful because: *nothing succeeds like mediocrity because everybody understands it so well.*"

As you can see, playing the fool is a lot of fun. It's also a great way to generate ideas and examine your most basic assumptions. While the ideas produced may not be immediately useful, it may happen that a foolish idea will lead to a practical, creative idea. And if you come up empty, at least you'll understand why the rule was there in the first place.

Summary

The fool's job is to shake, assault, massage, caress, and take a whack at the habits, rules, and conventions that keep you thinking the same old stuff. A good way to think of the fool is to compare your thinking to the transmission of a car. Most of the gears, like most thinking, are designed to go forward, to get ahead, to get the job done. But sometimes, when you can't make forward progress, you need to put it in reverse so that you can go forward anew. That's what the fool is all about: he's the reverse gear for your mind. He may not give you the right answer or solve your problem, but he'll get you out of the rut and put your thinking on a mental freeway where you might find a better solution yourself.

TIP: Occasionally, let your "stupid monitor" down, play the fool, and see what crazy ideas you can come up with.

9. To Err Is Wrong

Hits and Misses

In the summer of 1979, Boston Red Sox first baseman Carl Yastrzemski became the fifteenth player in baseball history to reach the three thousand hit plateau. This event drew a lot of media attention, and for about a week prior to the attainment of this goal, hundreds of reporters covered Yaz's every move. Finally, one reporter asked, "Hey Yaz, aren't you afraid all of this attention will go to your head?" Yastrzemski replied, "I look at it this way: in my career I've been up to bat over ten thousand times. That means I've been unsuccessful at the plate over seven thousand times. That fact alone keeps me from getting a swollen head."

Most people consider success and failure as opposites, but they are actually both products of the same process. As Yaz suggests, an activity that produces a hit may also produce a miss. It is the same with creative thinking. The same energy that generates good creative ideas also produces errors.

Many people, however, are not comfortable with errors. Our educational system, based on the "right answer" belief, cultivates our thinking in another, more conservative way. From an early age, we are taught that right answers are good and incorrect answers are bad. This value is deeply embedded in the incentive system used in most schools:

Right over 90% of the time = "A"
Right over 80% of the time = "B"
Right over 70% of the time = "C"
Right over 60% of the time = "D"
Less than 60% correct, you fail

From this we learn to be right as often as possible and to keep our mistakes to a minimum. We learn, in other words, that "to err is wrong."

With this kind of attitude, you aren't going to be taking too many chances. If you learn that failing even a little penalizes you (e.g., being wrong only 15% of the time garners you only a "B" performance), you learn not to make mistakes. And more important, you learn not to put yourself in situations where you might fail. This leads to conservative thought patterns designed to avoid the stigma our society places on "failure."

I have a friend who graduated from college with a master's degree in journalism. For six months, she tried to find a job, but to no avail. I talked with her about her situation, and realized that her problem was that she didn't know how to fail. She went through eighteen years of schooling without ever failing an examination, a paper, a midterm, a pop-quiz, or a final. So she was reluctant to try any approaches where she might fail. She had been conditioned to believe that failure is bad in and of itself, rather than a stepping stone to new ideas.

Look around. How many managers, housewives, students, teachers, congressmen, executives, musicians, and other people do you see who are afraid to try something new because of this fear of failure. Most of us have learned not to make mistakes in public. As a result, we remove ourselves from many learning experiences except for those occurring in the most private of circumstances.

A Different Logic

A man's errors are his portals of discovery.
—James Joyce, Author

From a practical standpoint, "to err is wrong" makes sense. Our survival in the everyday world requires us to perform thousands of small tasks without thinking about them. Think about it: you wouldn't last very long if you were to step out in front of traffic or stick your hand into a pot of boiling water. In addition, engineers whose bridges collapse, stock brokers who lose money for their clients, and copywriters whose ad campaigns decrease sales won't keep their jobs very long.

Nevertheless, too great an adherence to the belief "to err is wrong" can greatly undermine your attempts to generate new ideas. If you're more concerned with producing right answers than generating original ideas, you'll probably make uncritical use of the rules, formulae, and procedures used to obtain these right answers. By doing this, you'll by-pass the imaginative phase of the creative process, and thus spend little time testing assumptions, challenging the rules, asking what if, or just plain fooling around with the problem. All of these techniques will produce some incorrect answers, but in the imaginative phase errors are a necessary by-product of creative thinking. As Yaz would put it, "If you want the hits, be prepared for the misses." That's the way the game of life goes.

Whenever an error pops us, the usual response is "Jeez, another screwup, what went wrong this time?" The creative thinker, on the other hand, will realize the potential value of errors, and perhaps say something like, "Would you look at that! Where can it lead our thinking?" And then he or she will go on to use the error as a stepping stone to a new idea. As a matter of fact, the whole history of discovery is filled with people who used erroneous assumptions and failed ideas as stepping stones to new ideas. Columbus thought he was finding a shorter route to India. Johannes Kepler stumbled on to the idea of interplanetary gravity because of assumptions which were right for the wrong reasons. Thomas Edison knew 1,800 ways *not* to build a light bulb. Freud had several big failures before he developed psychoanalysis. One of Madame Curie's failures was radium.

Charles Kettering of General Motors, one of this century's great creative minds, had this to say about the value of learning to fail:

> An inventor is simply a person who doesn't take his education too seriously. You see, from the time a person is six years old until he graduates from college he has to take three or four examinations a year. If he flunks once, he is out. But an inventor is almost always failing. He tries and fails maybe a thousand times. If he succeeds once then he's in. These two things are diametrically opposite. We often say that the biggest job we have is to teach a newly hired employee how to fail intelligently. We have to train him to experiment over and over and to keep on trying and failing until he learns what will work.

Nature serves as a good example of how trial and error can be used to make changes. Every now and then genetic mutations occur—errors in gene reproduction. Most of the time, these mutations have a deleterious effect on the species, and they drop out of the gene pool. But occasionally, a mutation provides the species with something beneficial, and that change will be passed on to future generations. The rich variety of all species is due to this trial and error process. If there had never been any mutations from the first amoeba, where would we be now?

Is Failure Bad?

If you hit every time the target is too near or too big.
—Tom Hirshfield, Physicist

Your error rate in any activity is a function of your familiarity with that activity. If you are doing things that are routine for you, then you will probably make very few errors. But if you are doing things that have no precedence in your experience or are trying different approaches, then you will be making your share of mistakes. Innovators may not bat a thousand—far from it—but they do get new ideas.

Errors serve a useful purpose: they tell us when to change direction. When things go smoothly, we generally don't think about them. To a great extent, this is because we function according to the principle of negative feedback. Often it is only when things or people fail to do their job that they get our attention. For example, you are probably not thinking about your kneecaps right now. That's because everything is fine with them. The same goes for your elbows: they are also performing their function—no problem at all. But if you were to break a leg, you would immediately notice all the things you could no longer do, but which you used to take for granted.

Negative feedback means that the current approach is not working, and it is up to you to find a new one. We learn by trial and error, not by trial and rightness. If we did things correctly every time, we would never have to change course and we'd end up with more of the same.

After the supertanker *Exxon Valdez* broke open off of Alaska in the spring of 1989, thereby polluting the coast with millions of gallons of oil, the oil industry was forced to re-think and toughen up many of its safety standards regarding petroleum transport. The same thing happened after the accident at the *Three Mile Island* nuclear reactor in 1979—many safety standards were changed. The explosion of the *Challenger* space shuttle caused a similar thing to happen.

Neil Goldschmidt, former Secretary of Transportation, had

this to say about the [San Francisco] Bay Area Rapid Transit (BART):

> It's gotten too fashionable around the country to beat up on BART and not give credit to the vision that put this system in place. We have learned from BART. The lessons were put to use in Washington, in Atlanta, in Buffalo, and other cities where we've built mass transit systems. One of the lessons is not to build a system like BART.

I like to ask people if they've ever been fired from a job. If they have, they typically say something along the lines of, "Yeah, it was really traumatic when it happened, but it turned out to be the best thing that ever happened to me. It forced me to come to grips with who I was as a person. I had to look at my strengths and weaknesses with no delusions at all. It forced me to get out of my box and scramble. Six months later, I was in a much better situation."

We learn by our failures. A person's errors are the whacks that lead him or her to think something different.

Is Success Good?

This leads to another question: Is success a good thing? Sometimes the answer isn't so obvious. Just as it's possible that failure can lead to something good, sometimes success can lead to something bad. There are two ways in which this can happen.

First, success tends to lock you in a pattern, and you get the attitude, "If it's not broken, why fix it?" This attitude prevents you from experimenting and trying other approaches that in the long run may do you a lot more good.

Second, success—perversely enough—can create situations that undermine your original intentions and end up creating bigger problems than the ones you started with. Here are some examples:

◆ During the Soviet-Afghanistan war, the Soviets believed that their savage attacks on the civilian population would intimidate the Afghans into submission. Ironically, their attacks had just the opposite result. Because Afghan warriors historically stayed close to home to guard their women and children, the Soviets' driving Afghan dependents into refugee camps liberated the Mujahideen from their family responsibilities and turned them into more formidable opponents.

◆ In preparing for the Olympics, the coach of a leading crew team invited a meditation instructor to teach awareness techniques to his crew. He hoped that such training would enhance their rowing effectiveness and improve their sense of unity. As the crew learned more and more about meditation, they became more synchronized, their strokes got smoother, and there was less resistance. The irony is that their performance decreased and they went slower. It turned out that the crew was more interested in being in harmony than in winning. So the meditation teacher was dismissed.

◆ In the mid-1960's, the Japanese resort town of Atami lobbied hard to get a high-speed "bullet train" link to Tokyo, then three hours away. After the railway was completed, tourism declined–in part because the romance of going away for the weekend was lost in a place that could be reached in only fifty minutes.

◆ France's mobilization efforts in the first weeks of WWII were so successful that tens of thousands of key workers in vital war industries enlisted. As a result, these industries were practically brought to a halt, thereby placing the country at even greater risk. Several months later, the new recruits were returned to their jobs.

Is success good? Is failure bad? Well, like Yaz, I'd rather have a higher batting average than a lower one. Nonetheless, as I look back over my life, I find that I was successful at some

endeavors where I would have been better off had I failed.
That's because the success prevented me from experimenting
and trying different approaches. Conversely, there are places
where I'm glad I failed because it forced me to look for a second
right answer that, in hindsight, was much preferable to the
first.

Flex Your Risk Muscle

Strengthen your "risk muscle." Everyone has one. You keep
it in shape by trying new things. If you don't it atrophies and
you're no longer able to take chances. Make it a point to take at
least one risk every week. How can you exercise your risk
muscle today? Try a new recipe. Invest in a new idea. Tackle a
problem outside your field of expertise. As Arthur Koestler put
it: "If the Creator had a purpose in equipping us with a neck, he
certainly meant for us to stick it out."

Summary

There are places where errors are inappropriate, but the imaginative phase of the creative process isn't one of them. Errors are a sign that you are diverging from the well-traveled path. A large part of creative thinking is not being afraid to fail. As comedian/director Woody Allen put it, "If you're not failing every now and again, it's a sign you're not trying anything very innovative."

Remember these two benefits of failure. First, if you do fail, you learn what doesn't work. Second, the failure gives you an opportunity to try a new approach.

TIP: If you make an error, use it as a stepping stone to an idea you might not otherwise have discovered.

TIP: Differentiate between errors of "commission" and those of "omission." The latter can be more costly than the former. If you're not making many errors, you might ask yourself, "How many opportunities am I missing by not being more aggressive."

TIP: Before embarking on an idea or project, ask yourself: "What bad things can happen if we're successful?"

10. I'm Not Creative

Self-Fulfilling Prophecies

What concerns me is not the way things are, but rather the way people think things are.
—Epictetus, Philosopher

Several years ago, Johnny Carson made a joke on his television show that there was a toilet paper shortage in this country. He then went on to describe what some of the consequences of this shortage might be. The implication of this joke was that the viewers had better go out and stock up on toilet paper right away or else they would have to face these consequences. The subject made for a good laugh, since there was, in fact, no toilet paper shortage at all. Within days, however, a real shortage did develop. Because people thought there was a shortage, they went out and bought up all of the toilet paper they could find, and, as a result, they disrupted the normal flow of toilet paper distribution.

This serves as a good example of the self-fulfilling prophecy. This is the phenomenon whereby a person believes something to be true which may or may not be so, acts on that belief, and by his actions causes the belief to become true. As you can see, the self-fulfilling prophecy is a case where the world of thought overlaps with the world of action. And it happens in all avenues of life.

Business people are quite familiar with self-fulfilling prophecies. In fact, the whole notion of business confidence is based on them. If a business person thinks that the market is healthy (even though it may not be), he will invest money in it. This raises other people's confidence, and pretty soon the market will be healthy.

Educators are also aware of self-fulfilling prophecies. A few years ago, a teacher in New York was told that she had a class of gifted children, when in fact she had an ordinary class. As a result, she went out of her way to develop her students. She spent more time preparing her lessons and staying after class to give them ideas. The class, in turn, responded in a positive way, and scored higher than average on the same tests that previously had classified them as mediocre. Because they were treated as gifted children, they performed as gifted children.

This also happens in sales. Several years ago, I did a seminar with the direct sales force of a large pharmaceutical company. Prior to the session, I had an opportunity to talk to the people in the bottom 25% of sales performance. I asked them, "Why aren't you more successful?" They answered with such comments as:

"Our products cost too much."
"I've got a crummy territory."
"I don't get along with my manager."
"The moon is in Sagittarius."

What was their problem? They weren't taking responsibility for their own performance. They spent their time creating excuses rather innovative sales solutions.

I then talked to the top sales performers. These folks were happy, having fun, and achieving their goals. I asked them what the key to their success was. They said such things as:

> When I look at myself in the mirror in the morning, I see the face of an innovator. I see the face of a person who is going to accomplish wonderful things today. If I get turned down by a physician or a nurse, I think of a second way to get the business, a third way, and sometimes even a fifth way. I'm going to out-think the competition. I'm going to out-hustle the competition.

And that's the way it works out. It's a self-fulfilling prophecy. The same phenomenon is also found in athletics. I've noticed that one of the chief differences between winners and losers in athletic competition is that winners see themselves as

winning and losers generally give themselves a reason or an
excuse to lose. A person who exemplifies this is Bob Hopper, a
college teammate of mine at Ohio State in the mid-1960's. Bob
was an NCAA champion swimmer who rarely lost a race. One
day at the pool, I asked him why he was so successful at competitive swimming. He responded:

> There are several reasons. First, my strokes are all
> well-developed. Second, I work out hard. I've never
> "dogged" a workout in my life. Third, I take good care of
> myself and eat right. But my top competitors also do
> these things. So the key difference between just "being
> good" and "winning" is my mental preparation before
> each meet.
>
> Starting each day before the meet, I run the follow-
> ing movie through my mind. I see myself coming into
> the Natatorium, with three thousand cheering fans in
> the stands. I see the lights reflecting off the water. I can
> smell the chlorine, and feel the butterflies in my stom-
> ach. I see myself going up to the starting blocks. I see my
> competitors on each side. I hear the gun go off, and see
> myself diving into the pool and taking the first stroke of
> butterfly. I feel myself pulling through, then taking
> another stroke, and then another. I see myself coming
> to the wall, turning, and pushing off into the backstroke
> with a small lead. The lead gets bigger as I kick hard.
> Then I push off into the breaststroke. That's my best
> stroke and that's where I really open it up. Then I bring
> it home in the freestyle. I see myself winning!
>
> I run this movie through my mind twenty or thirty
> or forty times before each meet. When it comes time to
> swim, I just get in and win.

All of these examples demonstrate that just thinking a particular thought can have an enormous impact on the world of
action.

Give Yourself
A Creative License

Exercise: Are you creative? (Check the appropriate box.)

☐ Yes   ☐ No

Several years ago, a major oil company was concerned about the lack of creative productivity among its engineers. To deal with this problem, a team of psychologists was brought in to find out what differentiated the creative people from the lesser creative ones. They hoped that their findings could be used to stimulate the less creative people.

The psychologists asked the engineers all kinds of questions ranging from what their educational backgrounds were to where they grew up to what their favorite colors were. After three months of study, the psychologists found that the chief differentiating factor that separated the two groups was:

The creative people thought they were creative, and the less creative people didn't think they were.

As a consequence, the people who didn't think they were creative never put themselves in a position where they could use their creativity. They didn't allow themselves to get into an imaginative frame of mind, play with their knowledge, take a few risks, or look for the seventh right answer.

Some "I'm not creative" people stifle themselves because they think that creativity belongs only to the Einsteins, Curies, and Shakespeares of the world. To be sure, these are some of the superluminaries of the creative firmament, but by and large, these people didn't get their big ideas right out of the blue. On the contrary, most of their big ideas came from paying attention to their intermediate-size ideas, playing with them, and transforming them into big ideas. The same thing holds for most intermediate-size ideas. These come from small ideas which their creators paid attention to, and gradually worked into bigger things.

Thus, one of the major factors that differentiates creative people from lesser creative people is that creative people give themselves a license to pay attention to their small ideas. Even though they don't know where one of these will lead, they know that a small idea could lead to a big breakthrough, and they believe that they are capable of making it happen.

If you think you're creative, then you'll put yourself in situations where you can use your creativity, where you can take a few risks and try some new approaches, and where you come up with new ideas.

Summary

The worlds of thought and action overlap. What you think has a way of becoming true. If you want to be more creative, believe in the worth of your ideas, and have the persistence to continue building on them. With this attitude, you'll take more risks, and break the rules occasionally. You'll look for more than one right answer, explore for ideas outside your area, tolerate ambiguity, be foolish every now and then, play a little bit, engage in asking "what if" questions, and be motivated to go beyond the status quo. And finally, you'll be able to whack yourself into doing all of these things.

TIP: Whack yourself into trying new things and building on what you find—especially the small ideas. The creative person has the self-faith that these ideas will lead somewhere. And once you get an idea, do what you can to get the idea into action. Good luck!

Whack, whack, whack!

A Whack on the Other Side of the Head

The Student Returns
to the Creativity Teacher

Some people have ideas. A few
carry them into the world of
action and make them happen.
These are the innovators.
–Andrew Mercer, Innovator

A few months after his initial encounter with the creativity
teacher, the student returned to tell him of his progress.
"Things are really cooking," he said enthusiastically. "I've
opened up my mental locks, and I'm getting all kinds of ideas. I
take time to ask 'what if' and explore in outside areas. I used to
loathe problems, but now when they pop up, my mind dances
looking for opportunities. When I evaluate ideas, I try to use
even the stupidest ones as stepping stones to something new."

The teacher replied, "What are you going to do with these
new ideas?"

"I haven't really decided. But I'm getting ready to do something," he answered.

At this point, the teacher picked up a stick and gave him a
whack on the other side of the head. The student was stunned.
The teacher followed that act with this counsel: "Ideas are
great, but they aren't worth much if you don't use them. Now
you need to get your ideas into action. Here are some straightforward tips to help get the ball rolling."

Be Dissatisfied

An inventor was asked why he spent sixteen hours every day tinkering with his work. "Because I'm dissatisfied with everything as it currently exists in its present form." Dissatisfaction can be beneficial to the creative process. Otherwise you lose the prod you need to spot potential problems and opportunities. **What are you dissatisfied about? What are you going to do about it?**

Map Out Your Plans

What's your objective? What are you trying to accomplish?
Can you state it in a single sentence or two? Can you draw a
picture of it? Can you make a map of where you need to go and
the things you'll need to do? What planning do you need to do?
Can you visualize yourself reaching your objective?

Take A Whack At It

You can't hit a home run unless you step up to the plate. You can't catch fish unless you put your line in the water. You can't make your idea a reality unless you take a whack at it. Many of our personal goals are stranded on a little island called the "Someday I'll." Don't wait for your idea to happen. Make it happen. As adman Carl Ally put it, "Either you let your life slip away by not doing the things you want to do, or you get up and do them." If you want to be a singer, go sing. Sing in the shower. Sing for your friends. Join the choir. Audition for a musical. Start now. **What are three things you can do to reach your goal?**

Get Rid of Excuses

When the Spanish explorer Cortez landed at Vercruz, the first thing he did was burn his ships. Then he told his men: "You can either fight or die." Burning his ships removed a third alternative: giving up and returning to Spain. Sometimes it takes more creativity to get rid of the excuses we put in the way than it does to come up with the idea in the first place. **What three factors will make it difficult for you to reach your objective? How can you get rid of these excuses?**

Have Something at Stake

A frozen-fish processor had trouble selling a new line of frozen fish because it tasted "flat." The company tried to keep the fish fresh including holding them in tanks until just before processing—but to no avail. Then someone suggested: "Put a predator in there with them–that should keep them fresh." This idea worked like a charm. The fish kept moving and retained their vitality. Moral: have something at stake—survival, self-esteem, money, reputation—so that you'll be motivated to make your idea successful. **What do you have at stake?**

Get Support

One reason gypsies have a good health record is the role the family plays in establishing a positive health environment. When a gypsy gets sick, its not uncommon for six or eight other gypsies to accompany her to the doctor. Such family participation provides not only a support system for the ill member, it also creates a high expectancy for getting well. Similarly, it's much easier to be creative if your environment both supports and *expects* new ideas. **How can you create a support system around you?**

Sell, Sell, Sell

"It's not creative unless it sells," goes the advertising line. You can have the greatest idea in the world, but if you can't sell it, you won't get very far. What are three reasons that someone else would want you idea or product? What benefits does it provide? What does it promise? **How can you make your idea more attractive to other people?**

Be Courageous

"To fight a bull when you are not scared is nothing," says a well-known bull fighter. "And not to fight a bull when you are scared is nothing. But to fight a bull when you are scared—that is something." **What gives you the courage to act on your ideas? Having a well-thought out plan? Encouragement? Faith in your idea?**

Give Yourself A Deadline

Commercial jingle writer Steve Karmen once remarked, "The ultimate inspiration is the deadline. That's when you have to do what needs to be done." In a like vein, entertainment entrepreneur Nolan Bushnell has theorized that one thing that has made American business successful is what he calls the "Trade Show" phenomenon. As he puts it, "The fact that twice a year the creative talent of this country is working until midnight to get something ready for a trade show is very good for the economy. Without this kind of pressure, things would turn to mashed potatoes." **What tight deadline can you give yourself?**

Fight For It

"The only person who likes change is a wet baby," observes educator Roy Blitzer. Two basic rules of life are: 1) change is inevitable; and 2) everybody resists change. Much of the world has its defenses up to keep out new ideas. Thus, you need to become a warrior and do what's necessary to make your idea a reality. Sometimes, this means fighting your way past the obstacles you encounter. As Yoda the Jedi Warrior put it, "Try? There is no try. There is only do or not do." **What resistance do you expect to your idea? How can you overcome it? What are you willing to do to put your idea into action?**

Be Persistent

Once upon a time, two frogs fell into a bucket of cream. The first frog, seeing that there was no way to get any footing in the white fluid, accepted his fate and drowned.

The second frog didn't like that approach. He started thrashing around in the cream and doing whatever he could to stay afloat. After a while, his churning turned the cream into butter, and he was able to hop out. **How persistent are you?**

The student listened to all of this and said, "Thanks a lot. I appreciate your giving me these additional whacks. Now I can go out and get my ideas into action."

"You're welcome," said the creativity teacher. "Oh, yes, there's one more piece of advice I can give you."

"What's that?"

"After you implement your idea, give yourself a pat on the back. And then go out and earn another one."

Examination

Here's an opportunity to take some ideas from *A Whack on the Side of the Head* and carry them into action. Good luck!

1. Which (if any) of the mental locks prevent you from getting and using ideas?

☐ **The Right Answer.**

☐ **That's Not Logical.**

☐ **Be Practical.**

☐ **Follow the Rules.**

☐ **Play Is Frivolous.**

☐ **That's Not My Area.**

☐ **Avoid Ambiguity.**

☐ **Don't Be Foolish.**

☐ **To Err Is Wrong.**

☐ **I'm Not Creative.**

2. For those locks you checked, what things can you do to open them?

3. What is your creative thinking style?

A) How would your rate your ability as an *explorer?*
How frequently do you look for ideas in outside areas?

1	2	3	4	5	6	7	8	9	10
Never		Seldom			Sometimes			Often	

B) How would your rate your ability as a *magician?*
How frequently do you ask "what if" questions or use
impractical ideas as stepping stones to new ideas?

1	2	3	4	5	6	7	8	9	10

Never   Seldom   Sometimes   Often

C) How would your rate your ability as a *revolutionary?*
How frequently do you question assumptions, challenge
the rules, or discard obsolete ideas?

1	2	3	4	5	6	7	8	9	10

Never   Seldom   Sometimes   Often

D) How would your rate your ability as a *poet?* How frequently do you use soft thinking tools such as metaphors
and ambiguity to generate ideas?

1	2	3	4	5	6	7	8	9	10

Never   Seldom   Sometimes   Often

E) How would your rate your ability as a *fool?* How frequently do you reverse your point of view as a way of
breaking up groupthink situations?

1	2	3	4	5	6	7	8	9	10

Never   Seldom   Sometimes   Often

F) How would your rate your ability as a *warrior?* How
frequently are you able to motivate yourself, get rid of
excuses, and do what it takes in order to get your ideas
into action?

1	2	3	4	5	6	7	8	9	10

Never   Seldom   Sometimes   Often

4. What if the job you have ceased to exist tomorrow? What would you do? Think of three possibilities.

5. Propose to your boss (teacher, spouse, parent, leader, warden, etc.) that you spend one or two days in the next month doing some unusual activity. What would it be? What would make it worthwhile from his point of view, i.e., how would you sell it?

6. What are the three biggest errors you've made in the past five years? What were their beneficial consequences for you?

7. List three things you can do to flex your "risk muscle?" What is the most you can lose by taking these risks? What might you gain?

8. Each of us has myths about what we can't do: "I'm not good with numbers," "I could never learn how to cook," "I can't draw." These myths keep us from doing things we might learn from and enjoy. There are enough obstacles in the world without creating more. What personal myth can you explode?

9. Management consultant Peter Drucker was once asked by a person what skills he should learn in order to become a better manager. "Learn how to play the violin," he told him. What outside activity might you cultivate to make you more creative?

10. 17th century physician William Harvey compared the heart to a "pump" and then extended this metaphor to discover "blood circulation." Think of a concept you're developing. What can you compare it to? A raging river? A bud about to open? Building a house? Raising a child? Waging war? What similarities can you find?

11. "The time has come," the walrus said, "to talk of many things: of shoes—and ships—and sealing wax—of cabbages—and kings." Combining unusual ideas is at the heart of creative thinking. What different ideas can you combine?

12. Long ago, mapmakers sketched dragons on maps as a sign to sailors that they would be entering unknown territory at their own risk. Some sailors took this sign literally and were afraid to venture on. Others saw the dragons as a sign of opportunity, a door to virgin territory. Similarly, each of us has a mental map of the complete with dragons. Where does fear hold you back? What dragons can you slay?

13. Think up three captions for the illustration below.

14. Designer Scott Love has observed: "Only the most foolish of mice would hide in a cat's ear, but only the wisest of cats would think to look there." Don't miss the obvious. Ask yourself: "What resources and solutions are right in front of me?"

15. Poet Doug King on the value of incubating: "Learn to pause . . . or nothing worthwhile will catch up to you." Allow the Muse to whisper in your ear. What problem are you working on that would benefit from a pause?

16. Remember your models. When you were growing up, who were your models as creative people? A parent? A teacher or a coach? A friend? What advice would they give you today? What motivation would they give you? What kind of model are you?

17. Nothing magnifies your creative powers more than a clear sense of mission. He who puts in four hours of "want to" will almost always outperform the person who puts in eight hours of "have to." How can you convert your "have to's" to "can't wait to's"?

18. Software manager: "I like your program except for the ending." Programmer: "What's wrong with the ending?" Manager: "It should be closer to the beginning." What can you edit out of a current project to make it better? What can you simplify?

19. Many people live their lives fighting fires, tending routines, and letting events manage them rather than the other way around. Spend some time today engaged in fire prevention. What potential problems can you identify and remove?

20. Columbus challenged the Spanish courtiers to stand an egg on its end. They tried but failed. He then hard-boiled one and squashed it down. "That's not fair–you broke the rules," they protested. "Everything's fair after you've done it," he replied. What rules can you break in how you view a current problem?

21. Even the best lumberjack in the forest has to sharpen his axe. Spend a portion of your time analyzing your work methods. What new tools can you adopt? What new skills can you learn? What's out of date? What's a waste of your time? What can you do to make what you do more fun?

22. The ancients were amazed by two things beyond all else: the heavens above and their ability to procreate. What do you find amazing in life? Running water? Well-written books? Friendship? Jet travel? Computers? A good meal? What are two amazing things you can find today?

23. What is your number one goal? What are three factors that will make it difficult for you to reach this goal? Are you going to use these as excuses? How can you go over, under, around, or through these obstacles?

24. The days slip by. What were the two best ideas you has yesterday? Which ones did you act on? When you ask yourself these questions tomorrow, what will you say?

25. Let's go one step further. What will you be doing one year from today? What creative things will you have accomplished? What goals will you have reached?

About the Author
(The First Right Answer.)

Roger von Oech is the founder and president of Creative Think, a California-based company specializing in stimulating creativity through seminars, consulting, conferences, and products. His presentations and publications have stimulated the creativity of millions around the world.

Prior to starting Creative Think in 1977, he was employed by IBM in the areas of data base and data communications.

Dr. von Oech is a Phi Beta Kappa graduate from the Ohio State University where he received both the President's Scholarship Award and the Scholar-Athlete Award. He earned his doctorate from Stanford University in a self-conceived interdisciplinary program in the History of Ideas.

He is married to Wendy (who also works for Creative Think), and they have a daughter Athena and a son Alex.

About the Author
(The Second Right Answer.)

Sometimes I think the mind is like a compost pile. It contains a variety of ingredients all stewing together toward the ultimate end of producing something useful. Some ingredients aid the process, some hinder it, and others are inert.

Many of the ideas in my own compost heap have come from my work as a creativity consultant in industry. I picked up the other ingredients from a variety of experiences. My sixth grade teacher, Mr. Rodefer, taught me that being creative and being obnoxious are sometimes very similar, but that they are not the same thing. He taught me how to differentiate the two by giving me a creative license. We had an agreement: I'd run a lap around the school yard for every obnoxious act, and he would reward me for my new ideas. I learned to take chances. In addition to running 128 laps that year, I did some very creative things.

I learned about competition from swimming. I remember my sixteenth summer when Paul McCormick and I spent successive weeks beating each other's time in the 100 free. The competition made us both faster.

Some of my ideas came from hitchhiking around the country—I put over 30,000 miles on my right thumb in a five year period. I remember one ride in particular in which I learned about the economics of supply and demand. The driver was a Montana cowboy who was bootlegging pornography from San Francisco to Utah. He had discovered that there were people in the hinterlands who would pay three times the cover price for his four-color commodity.

As an undergraduate at Ohio State, I learned that someone from the corn belt could develop an appreciation for a culture twenty-five centuries long gone. In particular, I discovered the pre-Socratic philosopher Heraclitus who taught me that ambiguity can be a good thing when you're trying to generate new ideas.

I wrote my doctoral dissertation on the twentieth century German philosopher Ernst Cassirer, the last man to know everything. From him, I learned that it's good to be a generalist, and that looking at the Big Picture helps to keep you flexible.

Working for IBM taught me that there are a lot of hardworking, highly talented, narrowly focused people in the business world.

In having my own business, I discovered that you can have the greatest idea in the world, but if you can't sell it to other people, you're not going to get very far.

As the father of two children, I had it reinforced that we're all born with the ability to be creative and look at the world in different ways.

And in doing my own work, I've learned that people enjoy having their minds stimulated, and that a whack on the side of the head can be a positive experience.

Index of Proper Names

Alexander the Great 57
Woody Allen 160
Carl Ally 6, 173
St. Ambrose 136
Aslan the Dog 61
St. Augustine 136
Simon Ballantyne 127
Count Basie 26
Ludwig van Beethoven 58
Alexander Graham Bell 111
W.I. Beveridge 82
Roy Blitzer 180
Niels Bohr 44, 94, 118, 119, 140
Peter Borden 107
Kenneth Boulding 35
Georges Braque 108
Nolan Bushnell 106, 179
Samuel Butler 118
Audrey Joanne Caldwell 130
Diane Campbell 118
Johnny Carson 162
Ernst Cassirer 193
Emile Chartier 26
Winston Churchill 75
Christopher Columbus 154, 190
Nikolai Copernicus 58
Hernando Cortez 174
Marie Curie 155, 166
Edward de Bono 40
Owen Dennis 127
Walt Disney 76
Ray Dolby 29, 45
Peter Drucker 186
Thomas Edison 17, 109, 155
Albert Einstein 58, 77, 141, 166
Epictetus 162
Arthur Erickson 116
Rudolph Flesch 61
Frederick the Great 64
Sigmund Freud 40, 75, 155
Allen Funt 134

Ortega y Gasset 44
Neil Goldschmidt 156
Barbara Gorman 118
Jay Gould 17
Johann Gutenberg 6, 12
Franz Joseph Haydn 7, 12
William Harvey 187
Heraclitus 128, 130, 193
Tom Hirshfield 29, 60, 156
J. Edgar Hoover 114
Bob Hopper 164
Grace Hopper 6, 12, 116
Elias Howe 130
Eugene Ionesco 118
Edward Jenner 144
Jesus of Nazareth 49, 75, 92
Steve Jobs 46, 106
John the Baptist 91, 92
James Joyce 154
Steve Karmen 179
Alan Kay 118
Johannes Kepler 154
Kermit the Frog 128
Charles Kettering 155
Doug King 189
Martin Luther King 75
Arthur Koestler 159
Lao Tzu 91
Gary Laroff 94
Jerome Lawrence 86
Timothy Leary 119
Scott Love 189
Paul McCormick 191
Niccolo Machiavelli 75
Mao Zedong 111
Rex McPherson 18
Andrew Mercer 146, 170
Judy Massey 106
A.A. Milne 92
August Ferdinand Moebius 90
Frank Morrow 106

Napoleon Bonaparte 64, 111
John von Neumann 108
Isaac Newton 58
Richard Nicolosi 64
Nathan Olivera 106
George Patton 75, 116
Linus Pauling 28
Picasso 7, 12, 28, 84, 108, 116, 119
Alexander Pope 54
Neil Postman 23
Mario Puzo 112
Tom Robbins 78
Knute Rockne 108
John Rodefer 192
Agnew Spear Roe 97
Edward Armour Roe 97
John Roe 97
Merrill Lynmon Roe 97
Ernst Rommel 58
Sappho 58
Arthur Schnabel 118
Katherine Seligman 153
William Shakespeare 166

N.F. Simpson 119
Alfred Sloan 137
John Philip Sousa 55
The Three Stooges 75, 145
Simeon Stylites 127
Albert Szent-Györgyi 7
Mother Teresa 75
Arturo Toscanini 75
Mark Twain 66
Alex von Oech 135
Athena von Oech 130, 135
Wendy von Oech 130
George Wald 119
Paul Watzlawick 144
Bob Wieder 108, 119
Christopher Williams 144
Winnie the Pooh 91, 92
Wonder Woman 75
Xerxes 119
Carl Yastrzemski 152, 154
Yoda the Jedi Warrior 180
Your Mother 75

I hope you enjoyed this book. If you have any thoughts, comments, or creative experiences you'd like to share, I'd be delighted to hear from you.

Address all correspondence to me at:

> Creative Think
> Box 7354
> Menlo Park,
> California 94026
> USA
>
> Happy Whacking!
>
> R.v.O.